CHAT MATHS

INFORMAL HOMEWORK IDEAS FOR RECEPTION TO YEAR 6

by
Ruth Merttens,
Mary Boole,
Birmingham Primary School teachers,
and
members of Impact

Cover illustration by Iqbal Aslam
Other illustrations by Keith Grady

Birmingham
Advisory & Support Service
BASS

impact
MATHS HOMEWORK

Birmingham City Council
Education Service

UNIVERSITY OF
NORTH LONDON

Published by

Birmingham City Council
Education Service

Birmingham Advisory and Support Service,
Balden Road, Harborne, Birmingham B22 2EH.

June 2000

© Birmingham Advisory and Support Service,

ISBN 1–898244–48–0

Contents

Foreword by Tim Brighouse

Family involvement in education helps to raise standards and improve attitudes to learning. Homework can provide the opportunity for that involvement.

It is important that children see the relevance of the mathematics they learn in school to the outside world. Carefully planned homework can provide an opportunity for the transfer of that learning. Children's thinking skills and mathematical understanding can be sharpened by using them in different situations and with different people. When children have to articulate their thinking, they improve their communication skills, clarify their thoughts and extend their understanding. They can begin to evaluate when they need assistance and what kind, and it gives them a real-life setting in which to explore and discover.

Talking homework can also provide an opportunity for those at home to keep abreast of and be involved in their child's learning, whatever their literacy skills or language.

This book of homework activities for mathematics uses the context of the home and the local environment to set interesting, informal tasks using everyday items that are found in and around any home. But the purpose of every activity is clearly matched to objectives taken from the Framework for Teaching Mathematics. The section 'Back in school' gives credence to the homework task and further develops the interaction between home and school.

Everyone concerned with education – children, parents, carers and teachers – needs to recognise the value of this type of informal homework in the child's learning. We hope that you will find this book useful in helping to build those important bridges between education in and out of school.

Professor Tim Brighouse
Chief Education Officer,
Birmingham City Council

Introduction by Ruth Merttens

Homework and parental involvement

The National Numeracy Strategy stresses the importance of working with parents – and indeed, as it does so, it echoes the huge body of research and opinion which acknowledges the fact that parents are the single most important factor in children's educational success. Furthermore, primary schools are required to produce a policy on homework and to implement this policy. Most primary schools are already setting homework in English and maths, certainly for KS2 pupils, on a regular basis.

However, in linking these two things – homework and parental involvement – we always have to remember that homework serves a double function. It provides a mechanism whereby parents can get involved in the curriculum and in their children's learning. It also enables teachers to set extra work and allows them to reinforce the knowledge and understanding which has been introduced in class.

It is the first function – involving parents – which has the greatest impact on outcomes. Extra work can be set, and done, in school or in after-school clubs. But the involvement of parents, and the relation of the maths at school to the mathematics of everyday life, can only be achieved if these are explicitly on the agenda. And it is these which, if achieved, have a direct effect on children's educational attainment. Those children whose parents take an active interest in their learning are more likely to achieve their potential. And all children's mathematical understanding is increased by helping them to use the skills acquired in school in the home or the street.

This book is part of the endeavour to achieve both these aims. We need to ensure that homework consists, at least in part, of mathematical activities which are shared with a parent, older sibling, or other carer. Furthermore, we need to provide tasks that address the skills being taught at that time, and then locate their operation within non-school contexts. Thus, children can be encouraged to see the relevance of what they are learning and also to transfer skills from one context to another.

Teachers and homework

As a teacher, I find the whole business of setting homework and getting it back something of a nightmare. On top of an almost impossibly busy schedule, it is yet another thing to worry about, plan for and mark. It is also fraught with issues of equal access and opportunity. What do we do about the children who, seemingly, get no support at home and who never bring back their homework? How much pressure, morally speaking, can we put on children as they get older to do and deliver their homework? Do we set homework which reinforces the work being done in class, or should we use those commercially available homework books in which children run down a list of practice activities and keep a wide range of skills 'on the boil'? Should we set homework for children in KS1, or are they too young? How much homework is appropriate? All these questions, and others, are at the heart of the negative feelings which colleagues often express when discussing the topic.

As so often in education, the happiest solutions involve an element of compromise. We agree how we are going to set the homework, how often and what type. We decide which children we can fairly hassle about it and for which children pressure would be inappropriate or counter-productive. And we try to settle into a reasonable and comfortable routine of giving homework and following it up. Homework becomes another part of the process by which the Framework for Teaching Mathematics is followed and the curriculum implemented.

Informal homework

The essence of all the activities in this book is that they are informal. They take no preparation or photocopying, and they do not have to be marked! And precisely because of this informality, we can use these activities responsively. As we teach a particular topic we can flick through the book and decide if one of the informal homework activities is appropriate for this day's work.

This allows us to break out of the homework strait-jacket and react with a welcome degree of spontaneity to both our own teaching and to the children's responses. As we are teaching a particular topic, we can decide to ask the children to do something at home related to that topic, which will add to their understanding and probably involve their parent or carer.

In our experience, children's response to an informal homework activity often depends on how much value we, as teachers, place on what they bring back. To start with, some children may feel that because there is no workbook or piece of paper going home, this is not 'real' homework. But if their teacher makes a real fuss of any

feedback or product which comes back into school, children soon realise that this type of homework is as important as any other. Added to this is the fact that these informal homework activities are designed to be as much fun as possible!

Communicating with parents

The use of informal homework activities, as well as more traditional homework books or sheets, needs to be explained to parents as well as to the children. It is important to stress that most of the benefits of any type of homework are dependent upon the interest which the parents themselves show in what their children are doing. An informal homework activity which is shared with a parent, even where nothing is written down and no paper and pencil product results, is likely to be of far more value, mathematically speaking, than a page of sums where no one at home pays any attention.

Talking and learning

The talk that takes place as the child and the parent share the informal activity is where the learning takes place. Children come to be able to perform mathematical operations because they can talk themselves through them, and because they have the necessary vocabulary to make sense of what is going on.

The teachers and consultants who have written these activities are all teaching in classrooms and using these activities on a regular basis. This book has arisen out of the good ideas and practice of many teachers in Birmingham and in IMPACT. We hope you will enjoy using them and find them as useful as we do!

Ruth Merttens
Director of IMPACT

How to use this book

The activities in this homework book are all referenced to objectives in the National Numeracy Strategy Framework for Teaching Mathematics. They are set out in school years, Reception to Year 6, under the appropriate strand: Numbers and the number system, Calculations, Solving problems, Handling data and Measures, shape and space. The objectives referred to with each activity are in the order they appear in the Framework.

To find a task to set for homework, use the thumb index to find the appropriate year, then look for the strand, then the objective.

The tasks need no preparation or photocopying; instructions can be given to the children orally, though of course you may choose to tell them to write down certain things. For some tasks the children will need paper to record their work, but anything else they need can be found in and around their home.

As the activities do not need marking it is important that the children have a reason for doing their homework and that they see the value of it. So each activity has a corresponding section 'Back in school'. This gives you an idea of how you can follow up the task in the next lesson.

R E C E P T I O N
Counting and recognising numbers

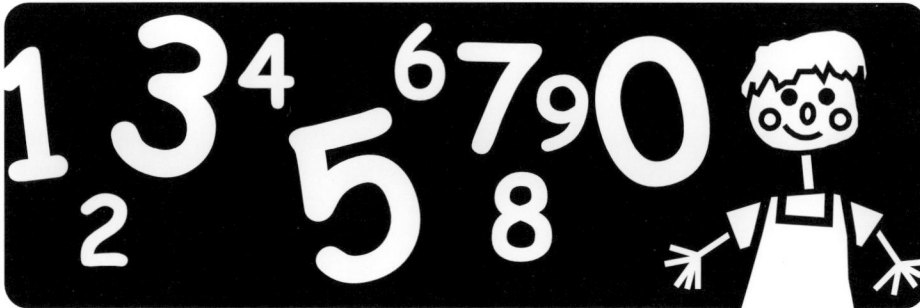

Objective
Counting and recognising numbers
Say and use the number names in order.

Instruction
Count the stairs as you go to bed.

Back in school
Count the steps from the door to your chair.

. . . .

Objective
Counting and recognising numbers
Count reliably up to 10 everyday objects.

Instruction
How many buildings can you see from your window? Try to count them. Remember the number to tell us in class.

Back in school
Compare the numbers of buildings. Write down their numbers. Discuss how you write each one.

. . . .

Objective
Counting and recognising numbers
Count reliably up to 10 everyday objects.

Instruction
Count the number of knives, forks and spoons you use at tea or supper.

Back in school
Compare the numbers of objects. Who used the most? How many are there in their family? Who used the least?

. . . .

Objective
Counting and recognising numbers
Count reliably up to 10 everyday objects.

Instruction
Count the number of coats which hang up in your home. Draw your own coat.

Back in school
Write down the numbers of coats. Compare their numbers and discuss who counted the most.

. . . .

Objective
Counting and recognising numbers
Count reliably up to 10 everyday objects.

Instruction
Look at all the lorries, vans or tractors you see as you go home. Look for the one which has the most wheels. How many wheels has it got? Draw a picture and bring it into school.

Back in school
Compare the numbers of wheels. Whose vehicle had the most? What type of vehicle was it?

Objective
Counting and recognising numbers
Count reliably up to 10 everyday objects.

Instruction
Count the number of coins in your mum's purse. Ask your mum to help draw around one of the coins and write the number that it says on it.

Back in school
Discuss the relative value of the amounts.

....

Objective
Counting and recognising numbers
Count reliably up to 10 everyday objects.

Instruction
Find out which of your clothes at home has the most buttons on it. Draw pictures to show what you have found.

Back in school
Compare the different numbers. Whose piece of clothing had the most buttons?

Objective
Counting and recognising numbers
Count reliably up to 10 everyday objects.

Instruction
How many things can you fit into a cup?

Back in school
Compare the numbers of objects. Who managed to fit the most things in their cup? What did they use?

....

Objective
Counting and recognising numbers
Count reliably in other contexts.

Instruction
Count the number of programmes you like to watch on TV. Draw a picture of your favourite programme and bring it into school.

Back in school
Discuss their favourite programmes and make a display. How many favourite programmes do we watch altogether?

....

Objective
Counting and recognising numbers
Count reliably in other contexts.

Instruction
Count the number of jumps you can do before you get tired! Ask someone to help you count and to write down the number of jumps.

Back in school
Discuss how many jumps they can do without getting tired. Choose a couple of children to jump while you count their jumps altogether!

....

Objective
Counting and recognising numbers
Count reliably in other contexts.

Instruction
Ask someone at home to clap their hands. You have to count the number of claps. Now you clap and they count!

Back in school
Repeat this process in class. Choose a child to clap whilst the rest of the class counts. This is quite hard!

. . . .

Objective
Counting and recognising numbers
Count reliably in other contexts.

Instruction
Ask someone in your house to click their fingers. How many times do they do this? You count! Now you try to click your fingers. How many times can you do this? They count!

Back in school
Repeat this process in class, choosing a child to click their fingers while the others count.

. . . .

Objective
Counting and recognising numbers
Count in tens.

Instruction
Count how many fingers and toes you have living in your house! E.g. Me: ten, twenty. Mum: thirty, forty. Fred: fifty, sixty... and so on. Count in tens and do not count above one hundred.

Back in School
Count in tens in the class. Choose ten children and count their fingers: ten, twenty, thirty....

Objective
Counting and recognising numbers
Count in twos.

Instruction
Line up several pairs of socks and count them in twos. How many socks?

Back in school
Discuss the different things we can count in twos and make a class list, e.g. socks, gloves, shoes.

. . . .

Objective
Counting and recognising numbers
Count in tens.

Instruction
Count in tens with someone in your house. Count up to one hundred and back. Think of something you could count in tens!

Back in school
Discuss the different things we can count in tens and make a class list, e.g. packets of 10 biscuits, finger puppets.

. . . .

Objective
Counting and recognising numbers
Recognise and begin to record numerals.

Instruction
See what numbers you can see around your home, on your clock, cooker, door, etc.

Back in school
Look around the school. Are there numbers on any doors?

. . . .

Objective
Counting and recognising numbers
Recognise and begin to record numerals.

Instruction
Make a number frieze for your bedroom. Include the numbers 1-10 and draw or write something special to go with each one, e.g. I have 3 cats. I am 4 years old.

Back in school
Make a number frieze for the class. Each child makes their own number special – one number per child.

. . . .

Objective
Counting and recognising numbers
Recognise and begin to record numerals.

Instruction
Write your favourite number. Write it large on a piece of paper. Decorate it nicely.

Back in school
Display their numerals and match them to beads, beans, bricks, or other small objects.

. . . .

Objective
Counting and recognising numbers
Recognise and begin to record numerals.

Instruction
Write your name carefully. Count the number of letters. Write the number next to your name and bring it back to school.

Back in school
Make a book of the children's names, organising the book according to the number of letters in their names. Have a number on a page, and then all the names with that many letters around it.

. . . .

Objective
Counting and recognising numbers
Recognise and begin to record numerals.

Instruction:
Write the numbers up to 5. Find a person or pet that you know whose age is each number and draw them beside their number.

Back in school:
Make a display of all the children's drawings, writing the names of their friends or animals beside their drawings.

Objective
Counting and recognising numbers

Comparing and ordering numbers – order a given set of selected numbers

Instruction
Ask someone to help you write down the ages of several people in your family. Write each age on a small piece of paper. Put the ages in order, youngest to oldest! Stick them on another piece of paper and bring them back to school.

Back in school
Discuss the numbers they wrote down. Talk about which numbers are largest and which are smallest. Match some of the numbers to the 0-99 or 1-100 number grid.

· · · · · · · ·

Objective
Counting and recognising numbers

Comparing and ordering numbers – begin to understand and use ordinal numbers in different contexts.

Instruction
Ask someone what day of the month you were born on. Try to remember it! Write it down and bring it into school.

Back in school
Compare their numbers. Which numbers are less than ten? Which are more than ten? Which are less than twenty? Etc.

· · · · · · · ·

Objective
Counting and recognising numbers

Comparing and ordering numbers – use language such as more or less, greater or smaller to compare two numbers.

Instruction
Write down your favourite number and someone else in your home's favourite number. Bring them both into school.

Back in school
Compare their two numbers. Each child has to say which number is larger. Which numbers are less than ten? Which are more than ten? Which are less than twenty? Etc.

My house number is 8... what's yours?

Objective
Counting and recognising numbers

Comparing and ordering numbers – use language such as more or less, greater or smaller.

Instruction
Look at your house number. Copy it down and bring it into school.

Back in school
Compare their numbers. Which numbers are less than ten? Which are more than ten? Which are less than twenty? Etc.

· · · · · · · ·

Adding and subtracting numbers

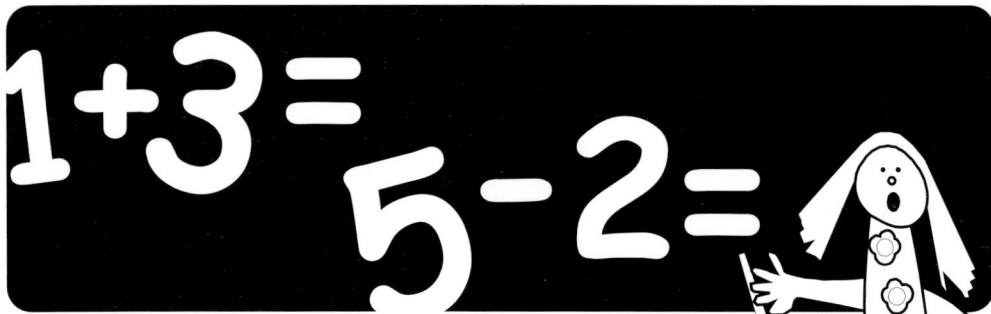

$1+3=$
$5-2=$

Objective
Adding and subtracting numbers
Find one more than a number up to 10.

Instruction
Ask someone to help you to write the number which is one more than your house number. Bring it into school.

Back in school
Use the children's numbers to try to work out each person's house number. Look along the number line or grid to find one less!

. . . .

Objective
Adding and subtracting numbers
Find one more than a number up to 10.

Instruction
Write the number which is one more than your age. If you like, write the number which is one more than someone else's age!

Back in school
Write down the children's ages. Look along the number line. Check which number is one more. Match the other numbers they found to the number line or grid, and check which number is one more.

. . . .

Objective
Adding and subtracting numbers
Begin to add by counting on.

Instruction
Throw a dice. Say the number which is one more. If you are right, have a raisin or Smartie! Now let your partner have a turn.

Back in school
Repeat the game in class. Throw the dice. The children have to say the number which is one more. Encourage them to use a number line to help them. Divide the children into teams and play.

Objective
Adding and subtracting numbers
Begin to add by counting on.

Instruction:
Throw a dice. Say the number which is two more. If you are right, have a raisin or Smartie! Now let your partner have a turn.

Back in school
Repeat the game in class. Throw the dice. The children have to say the number which is two more. Encourage them to use a number line to help them. Divide the children into teams and play.

. . . .

Objective
Adding and subtracting numbers
Find a total by counting on when one set is hidden.

Instruction
Use a tea-towel or cloth. Lay out a line of 6 (or 7, or 8, or 9...) mugs. Cover one part of the line with the cloth. Count how many mugs are visible, by pointing at each one. Then remove the cloth and count how many there are in all by counting on. Check your total!

Back in school
Repeat the game in class. Use the number line. The children have to count on from the visible number to the total.

. . . .

Objective
Adding and subtracting numbers.
Separate (partition) a given number of objects into two groups.

Instruction
Arrange six biscuits or sweets on two plates. How many different ways can you arrange them? Ask someone to help you write them down.

Back in school
Write down the number sentences to match their arrangements. 1 + 5, 2 + 4, etc. Use large bricks to demonstrate that it is always six!

Repeat this activity for five objects or for seven objects!

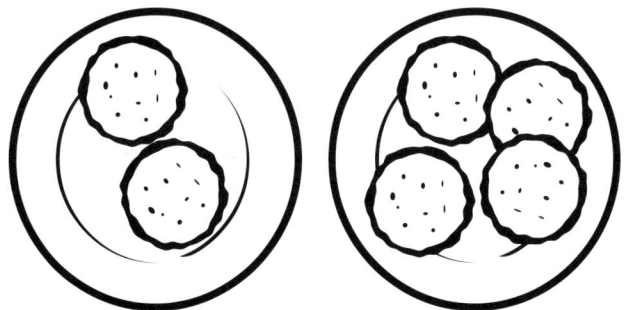

Solving problems

how do I...

Objective
Solving problems
Sort and match objects.

Instruction
Lay the table at home – plates first, then forks, knives, etc., one for each person.

Back in school
Give every child in the class a pencil. How many pencils are there?

. . . .

Objective
Solving problems
Sort and match objects.

Instruction
Choose a colour and draw as many things as you can find in your house which are that colour.

Back in school
Discuss the most common colour chosen.

. . . .

Objective
Solving problems
Sort and match objects.

Instruction
Choose a shape and then draw as many things as you can find in your house which are that shape.

Back in school
Discuss the most common shape found.

. . . .

From 'The Pines' School

Objective
Solving problems
Begin to understand and use the vocabulary related to money.

Instruction
Find a label or ticket with a price on it. Bring it into school.

Back in school
Discuss the amounts of money on the labels. Categorise the amounts: less than 50p, more than 50p, less than £1, more than £1, less than £10, more than £10.

Measures, shape and space

Objective
Measures, shape and space
Use language to compare more than two quantities.

Instruction
Draw a picture of your family from the tallest to the shortest.

Back in school
Display the drawings under the number of people shown in each picture.

. . . .

Objective
Measures, shape and space
Begin to name flat shapes such as circle, triangle, square, rectangle....

Instruction
Look at the shape of the windows in your house. What shapes can you see?

Back in school
Discuss the most common shape for windows in the home. Is that the same at school?

Objective
Measures, shape and space
Begin to name flat shapes such as circle, triangle, square, rectangle.

Instruction
Look for street signs that are 2D shapes. What shapes can you see and what do you see written on them? Ask an adult what they mean. Do a drawing of one of the ones you have spotted and bring it to school.

Teacher's note: circles are used a lot for signs e.g. upper speed limit signs. Road names are usually rectangular signs. Triangles are warning signs.

Back in school
Collect the drawings and display them under the shape name headings.

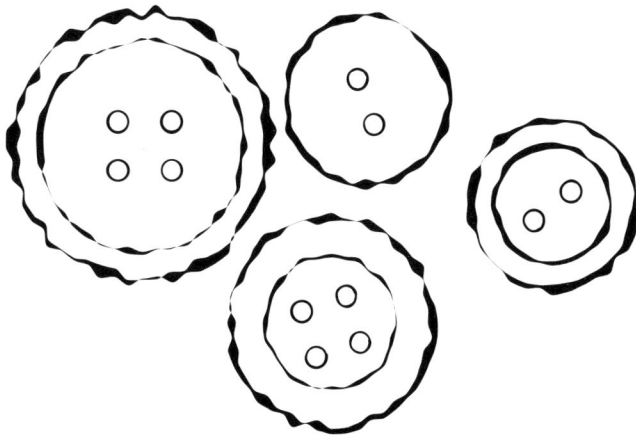

Objective

Measures, shape and space

Use a variety of shapes to make pictures and patterns.

Instruction

Find some buttons or coins at home. Ask someone to help you draw around some to make a pattern and bring it into school.

Back in school

Discuss different patterns. Count the numbers of objects used.

. . . .

From Anne Higgins, St Alban's RC Primary School

Objective

Measures, shape and space

Begin to name solid shapes.

Instruction

Look for some cubes, cones, spheres or other 3D shapes at home. Bring one of the objects in or draw a picture of it. The class will then look at and identify the shapes.

Back in school

Children can build structures using their shapes.

. . . .

YEAR 1
Numbers and the number system

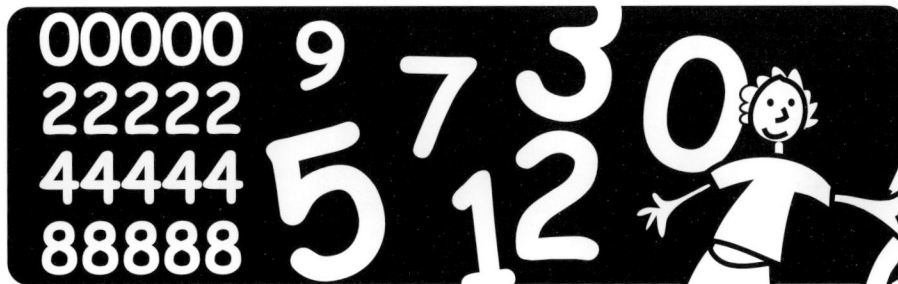

00000 9 7 3 0
22222 5 12
44444
88888

Objective
Numbers and the number system
Count reliably at least 20 objects.

Instruction
Find someone to work with. Ask them to turn out their pockets or empty their purse! Count how many coins there are. Which coin is largest? Which coin is worth the most?

Back in school
In class, look at different (real) coins. Which one is largest? Is that one worth the most? What can you buy for £2?

....

Objective
Numbers and the number system
Count reliably at least 20 objects.

Instruction
Find someone to play with! Take a handful each of dried beans or small pasta pieces. Guess first how many you have. Now count carefully each handful. Whose guess was closest? Play again.

Back in school
In class, play using small beads or cubes, teacher against class! Take a cupful, estimate first and then count. Stress that to count accurately, we group them in fives and tens as we count.

Objective
Numbers and the number system
Count reliably to 20 and beyond.
Count on and back from any small number.

Instruction
Make up your own number rhyme. Remember that you could count forwards or backwards.

Back in school
The children can tell you their number rhymes. Write them down, polish them up and make a class book of number rhymes. Each day, use a different one!

Objective
Numbers and the number system
Count reliably to 20 and beyond.
Count on and back from any small number.
Count on or back in tens from and to zero.

Instruction
Count in tens from 0 to 100. Make up a rhyme to go with each number! E.g. Ten, hen. Twenty, empty. Thirty, dirty. Forty, naughty, etc.

Back in school
The children can tell you their number rhymes. Write them down, polish them up and make a class book of number rhymes. Each day, use a different one!

. . . .

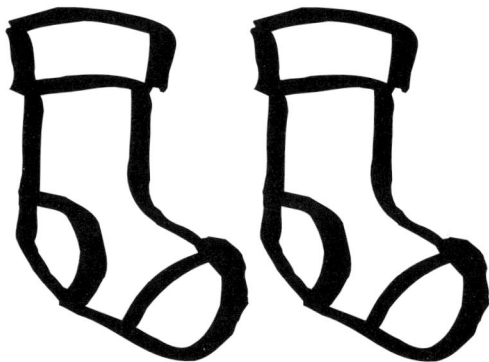

Objective
Numbers and the number system
Count in twos.

Instruction
Look for pairs of things in your house. Draw pictures of them. Give an example through illustration.

Back in school
Discuss the fact that we talk about 'a pair of socks' – 2 socks, and also a 'pair of pants' – 1 item of clothing, and why that might be.

. . . .

Objective
Numbers and the number system
Count in twos from zero.
Read and write the numerals to at least 20.

Instruction
Count in twos with someone else in your house. Write each number you say. Can you think of a rhyme, e.g. 2, moo. 4, door. 6, mix, etc.

Back in school
In class, make an even number display with all their rhymes.

. . . .

Objective
Numbers and the number system
Count reliably at least 20 objects.
Understand the vocabulary of comparing and ordering numbers.

Instruction
Count the number of forks you have in your house. Then count the number of knives you have. Then count the number of spoons. Write down the numbers and say which you have the most of.

Back in school
Discuss and compare different numbers. Which is the largest? Which is the smallest?

. . . .

Objective

Numbers and the number system

Count reliably at least 20 objects.
Read and write the numerals to at least 20.

Instruction

Look for an article of clothing in your house which has lots of buttons. How many buttons does it have? Count the buttons carefully and write the numbers. Draw the article of clothing.

Back in school

In class, sort their drawings according to the numbers of buttons and make a button number frieze.

. . . .

Objective

Numbers and the number system

Read and write the numerals to at least 20.

Instruction

Find someone at home to work with. Write a number with your finger on their back. Do it very carefully, remembering to start at the top. Can they say what number you are writing? Now let them write a number with their finger on your back.

Back in school

In class, put the children in pairs and let them play this game. The children work in pairs sitting so that one person has their back to the board. Write a number on the board. The other child writes that number on that child's back. Can they say what it is? Now the children swap round and you write another number on the board.

Objective

Numbers and the number system

Count reliably to 20 and beyond.
Read and write the numerals to at least 20.

Instruction

Find someone at home to work with. Make a number track at home, writing the numbers in each space. Make it as long as you like! Play a game, spinning a coin and moving two spaces for heads and three for tails. Who is the first to reach the end of your track?

Back in school

In class, put the children in pairs and allow them to play their track games.

. . . .

Objective

Numbers and the number system

Begin to know what each digit in a two-digit number represents.

Instruction

On your way home look for a number with a 6 in the tens place.

Back in school

Choose different children to come and write numbers they saw. Are all these appropriate? Extend by asking children to think of a number that has a 6 in the tens place and a 6 in the units place.

. . . .

From 'The Pines' School

Objective
Numbers and the number system
Compare two familiar numbers and say which is more or less.

Instruction
What is the largest number you can see on your way home?
What is the smallest?

Back in school
Discuss where the children saw their largest and smallest number. Can they find the numbers on the number grid?

. . . .

Objective
Numbers and the number system
Compare two familiar numbers and give a number that lies between them.

Instruction
Write down the number of your home. Then write down the number of your friend's home. Then write down a number that comes between these numbers.

Write down your age. Then ask someone in your home their age. Write it down. Then write down a number that comes between these numbers. Do that with two other people in your family.

Back in school
Write down two ages and compare them. Find the ages on the number grid.

Objective
Numbers and the number system
Give a sensible estimate of a number of objects that can be checked by counting.

Instruction
Guess how many sweets are in the packet before you open it. Then count them. How close were you?

Back in school
Bring in a jar of biscuits. (Small savoury ones are good!). The children guess first and then count. Stress that we group in fives and tens to count effectively.

. . . .

Objective
Number and the number system
Understand and use the vocabulary of estimation.
Give a sensible estimate of a number of objects that can be checked by counting.

Instruction
Draw around your hand. Choose some small objects that you can put on there. (Teachers may want to be more specific and suggest for example 1p/2p coins, dried pasta shapes, paper clips, etc. They might want some groups of children to use some things and other groups other things.)

Estimate the number of small objects that can fit on there. Write that number on your drawing. Then see how many of those objects you can fit on. Write down the number. If you've only got one 1p coin for example you could keep drawing around the one you've got. Make sure they all touch each other.

Demonstrate this activity in class so the children understand how easy it is. This activity can be repeated another night when they can draw around an adult's hand.

Back in school
Draw round a foot. Use the same object to cover it and compare the number with the hand.

Calculations

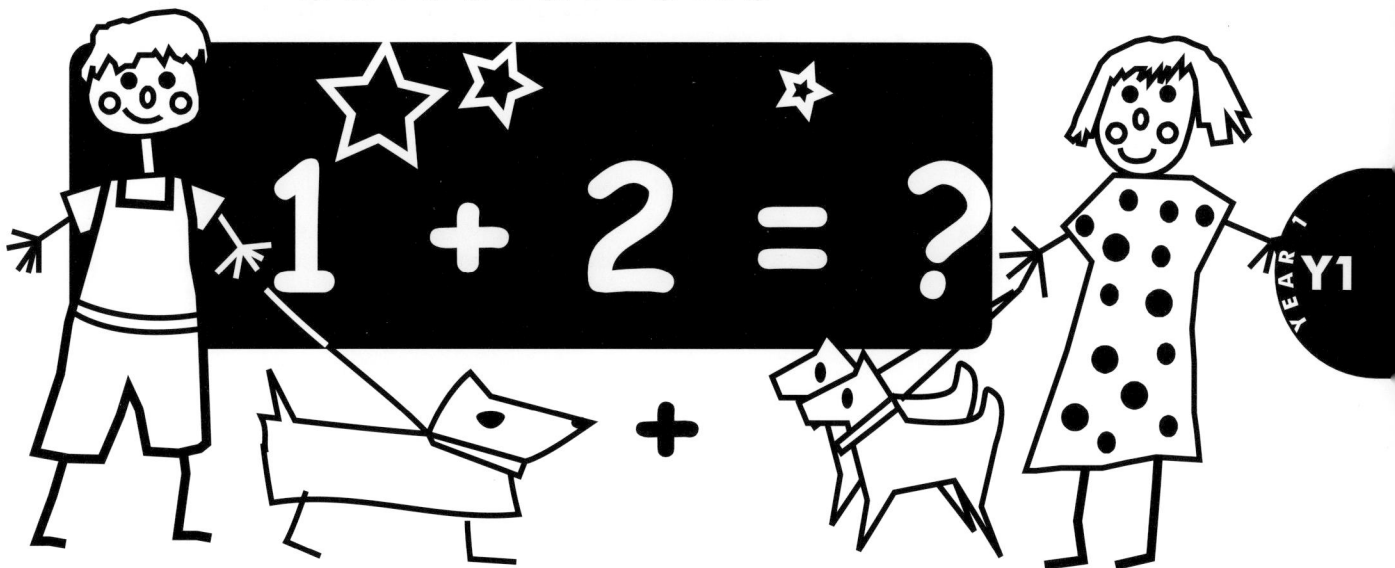

1 + 2 = ?

Objective
Calculations

Understand the operation of addition and related vocabulary.

Instruction
Make up a story where you would need to add to find the answer, e.g. I've got three pets and my friend has got two. How many have we got altogether? Ask someone at home to help you write it.

Back in school
Compare lots of stories. Make up a class story with big numbers.

. . . .

Objective
Calculations

Understand the operation of subtraction and related vocabulary.

Instruction
Make up a story where you would need to subtract to find the answer, e.g. Mum bought 10 apples and put them in the fruit bowl. Then I ate one. How many are left in the bowl? Ask someone at home to help you write it.

Back in school
Compare lots of stories. Make up a class story.

From Paul Tremere

Objective
Calculations

Begin to recognise that more than two numbers can be added together.

Instruction
Ask someone at home to take three small plates or saucers from the kitchen cupboard. Find ten small objects, such as one penny coins, buttons or something like that. Put the objects onto the plates and write down how you did it. For example:
5 + 3 + 2 = 10

Ask the adult to rearrange the objects on the plates and then write down how they did it. Bring your sums to school.

Back in school
Things to think and talk about:
Can you have an empty plate, or two? Use zero?
Does the order of the plates matter? (Is 1 + 4 + 5 + the same as 5 + 1 + 4 or even 4 + 5 + 1? Look at the plates from the other side of the table!)
Keep a fixed amount on one of the plates and change the other two eg 4 + 2 + 4 or 4 + 3 + 3 or 4 + 5 + 1.

. . . .

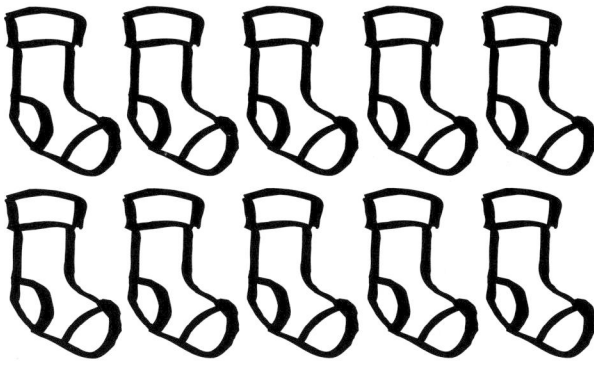

Objective
Calculations
Know by heart all pairs of numbers with a total of 10.

Instruction
Take 10 socks. How many different ways can you make two piles e.g. 3 + 7 = 10. Write down the number sentence for each way. Bring your sums back into class.

Back in school
Write down all the possible number sentences for ten, e.g. 5 + 5 = 10, 6 + 4 = 10, etc.

. . . .

From Paul Tremere

Objective
Calculations
Begin to know addition facts for all numbers with a total up to at least 10, and the corresponding subtraction facts.

Instruction
Put ten objects into a bag. Take it in turns to play. One person takes some out of the bag and shows them. The other person decides how many objects are left in the bag. Count them to check if you are right!

Back in school
The children can play the same activity with 8 objects in a bag.

. . . .

Objective
Calculations
In addition, put the larger number first and count on in ones.

Instruction
Write down your age. Talk to someone at home. Write down their age. Can you add the two numbers together?
Write down the total. Bring it into school. Do the same with two other people in your family.

Back in school
Work out the other person's age!

. . . .

Solving problems

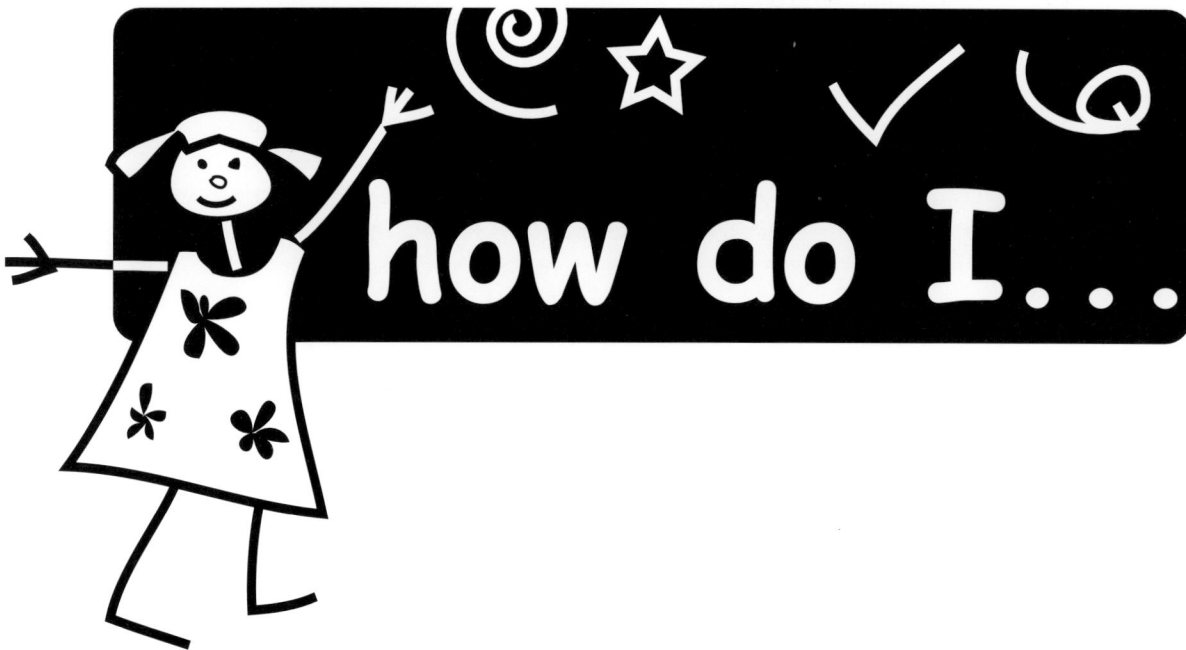

how do I...

Objective
Solving problems

Solve simple word problems and explain how the problem was solved.

Instruction
Fold a piece of paper in half. On the outside write a 'think of a number' problem e.g. I'm thinking of a number. I add 3. The answer is 10. What was my number? Then write what the number was on the inside, e.g. 7.

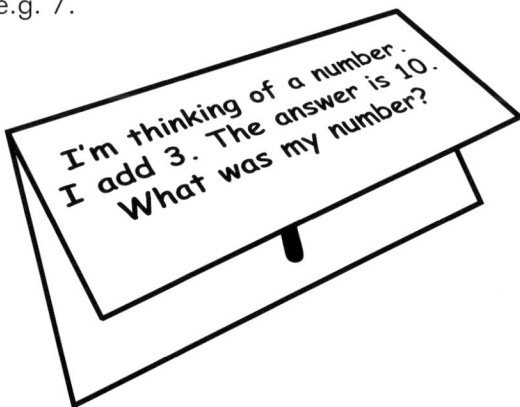

I'm thinking of a number. I add 3. The answer is 10. What was my number?

Back in school
Divide the children into pairs. They make their own 'think of a number' problem and play with each other.

. . . .

From Paul Tremere

Objective
Solving problems

Solve simple mathematical problems and suggest extensions.
Begin to recognise that more than two numbers can be added together.

Instruction
Imagine that there is a target painted on a wall. It has 5 and 3 painted on it. You can throw three balls at the target. What totals could you score, e.g. $5 + 5 + 3$?

Back in school
Use two new numbers. What could you score now? Put the scores in order, smallest to biggest.
Add up the possible scores to find a grand total. Is there a quicker way of finding this total?

. . . .

Objective
Solving problems
Recognise coins and notes of different values.

Instruction
Ask someone at home for some coins. Can you make 10p from the coins they have? Draw round the coins you used. (The children can make 5p or 20p if it is more appropriate).

Back in school
Look at all the different ways of making 10p. Record these on a flip chart.

. . . .

Objective
Solving problems
Work out how to pay an exact sum using smaller coins.

Instruction
Draw your favourite sweet. Ask your mum or carer how much it costs. Then draw a price label on it. Draw what coins you would use to pay for it.

Back in school
Compare the prices of different sweets.

. . . .

Measures, shape and space

Objective
Measures, shape and space
Compare two lengths by direct comparison.

Instruction
Compare the lengths of two similar pieces of cutlery, e.g. big spoon, little spoon. Place one beside the other. Draw round them both.

Back in school
Compare the lengths of several different spoons (ladle, tablespoon, desert spoon, teaspoon, etc.)

Objective
Measures, shape and space
Compare two heights by direct comparison.

Instruction
Compare the heights of two things, e.g. two chairs, or two cupboards. Draw them both.

Back in school
Make two class books - a 'tall things' book and a 'short things' book, using the children's drawings.

Objective
Measures, shape and space
Compare two capacities by direct comparison.

Instruction
Compare the capacities of two mugs. Fill one mug with water and pour it carefully into the other mug. Does it fill it up – and perhaps overflow? Repeat this, filling the second mug and pouring it into the first. Decide which mug holds most and draw it.

Back in school
Repeat this in class, finding the difference between two of the staffroom mugs! Which teacher's mug is the largest? Who drinks the most coffee?!

. . . .

Objective
Measures, shape and space
Compare two weights by direct comparison.

Instruction
Compare the weights of two things of similar size, e.g. a book and a box of paper hankies, a mug and a loo roll. Draw round them both.

Back in school
Compare the weights of several different things which are all about the same size. Use some that the children chose and place them on the balances.

Objective
Measures, shape and space
Suggest suitable units to measure the length of an object.

Instruction
Draw round your foot. Find some small objects (e.g. small pasta pieces, dried beans, Lego bricks...) to lie along your drawing. How long is your foot? Guess first, then lie the objects along its length and count them. Write the number and bring your drawing into class.

Back in school
Discuss what they used to measure their feet. Display their drawings and stick some of the units they used on the display.

. . . .

Objective
Measures, shape and space
Suggest suitable units to measure the length of an object.

Instruction
Draw round your favourite toy. Find some small objects (e.g. small pasta pieces, dried beans, Lego bricks...) to lie along your drawing. How long is your toy? Guess first, then lie the objects along its length and count them. Write the number and bring your drawing into class.

Back in school
Discuss what they used to measure their toys. Make a class book using their drawings. Help them to write a sentence describing each toy, using mathematical language.

. . . .

Objective
Measures, shape and space
Suggest suitable units to measure the length of an object.

Instruction
Ask someone if you can hold the phone. Draw round it. Find some small objects (e.g. small pasta pieces, dried beans, Lego bricks...) to lie along your drawing. How long is the phone? Guess first, then lie the objects along its length and count them. Write the number and bring your drawing into class.

Back in school
Discuss what they used to measure the phone. Was the phone longer than it was wide? Discuss different phone shapes.

. . . .

Objective
Measures, shape and space
Understand and use the vocabulary related to time.

Instruction
Find out the time of your favourite programme. Write it down and bring it into school.

Back in school
Discuss the times. Categorise them, morning, afternoon, evening. Which ones are on an 'o'clock'?

. . . .

From Helen Leach, St Albans RC Primary School

Objective
Measures, shape and space
Use everyday language to describe features of familiar 3D and 2D shapes.

Instruction
See how many different flat and solid shapes you can find in your home, e.g. a tin is a cylinder, a paper tissue could be a square. Draw some of these shapes.

Back in school
Children report back at the beginning of next 'shape' lesson to the class and use solid shapes and 2D shapes to illustrate their findings.

Y1 YEAR 1

YEAR 2
Numbers and the number system

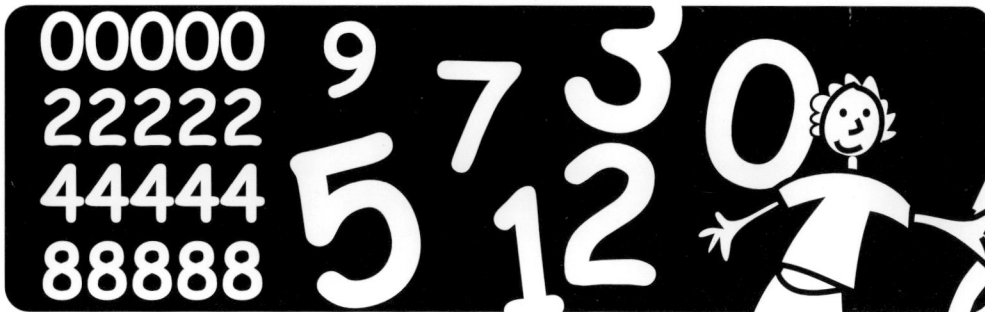

```
00000  9 7 3 0
22222  5 1 2 0
44444
88888
```

Objective
Numbers and the number system
Count reliably up to 100.

Instruction
Count the number of steps you walk to get home! This may be quite hard!

Back in school
Write all the numbers the children have counted. Some of them may have given up! What was the highest number they got to? Compare their numbers.

. . . .

Objective
Numbers and the number system
Count reliably up to 100 objects.

Instruction
Count the number of cars you see on your way home. Write the total number and draw your favourite car!

Back in school
Order the number of cars the children counted from smallest to largest and put them in a class book.

. . . .

Objective
Numbers and the number system
Count reliably up to 100 objects by grouping.

Instruction
Find something that you can count out one hundred of, e.g. dried beans, small pasta pieces, Lego bricks. Count out one hundred very carefully (grouping in tens as you go) – and ask someone else to check. Did you do it right?

Back in school
The children work in pairs to count one hundred of something in class. What did they count at home? Try to choose the same objects.

Objective
Numbers and the number system
Count reliably up to 100 objects by grouping.

Instruction
Collect together fifty small objects in a bag and bring them into school. There must be exactly 50!

Back in school
The children work in pairs. Now they have one hundred things. They can count them carefully together, grouping their objects in tens. Discuss the things they chose to put in the bag!

. . . .

Objective
Numbers and the number system
Recognise odd and even numbers.

Instruction
Write down your house number and your next door neighbours' house numbers (both sides).
Are they odd or even numbers?

Teacher's note: If some children live in flats or cul-de-sacs the numbering system might be different from that of a street. This could promote discussion.

Back in school
Discuss whose house or flat number is the largest? Is it even or odd? Whose is the smallest? Is it even or odd?

. . . .

Objective
Numbers and the number system
Begin to recognise two-digit multiples of 2, 5 and 10.

Instruction
Find out the ages of five people in your family. (They don't have to live in your house.) Draw a circle round the ones that are multiples of 2 or 10.

Back in school
Write all the multiples of 10 the children have found. What do we notice? Repeat for multiples of 2.

. . . .

Objective
Numbers and the number system
Begin to recognise the multiples of 2, 5 and 10.

Instruction
Find someone to play with! Throw two dice. Arrange the numbers to make a two-digit number. Take 2 points if it is in the two's count. Take 5 points if it is in the five's count. Now let your partner have a turn. Play until one person collects 20 points.

Back in school
Repeat the game in class, playing teacher against the class!

. . . .

Objective
Numbers and the number system
Use the vocabulary of estimation and approximation.

Instruction
Find a leaf with about 20 veins on it. What about one with 50 veins on it?

Back in school
Compare leaves. How can we estimate the number?

From Paul Tremere

Objective

Numbers and the number system
Read whole numbers to at least 100.

Instruction
Look at the figures on a car number plate.

Arrange the figures to make different numbers. Make a list of the numbers and say them out loud to someone at home. Say them as whole numbers, e.g. for 634 say 'Six hundred and thirty four'.

Back in school
The children work in pairs to put the numbers in order, starting with the smallest.

· · · · · · · ·

Objective

Numbers and the number system
Compare two two-digit numbers, say which is more or less and give a number in between them.

Instruction
Write down the name and age of the oldest person you know. Then write down the name and age of someone who is much younger. Then write down the age of someone whose age is between those two.

Back in school
How old is the oldest person? Find that number on the number grid. How long before they are 100?

· · · · · · · ·

Objective

Numbers and the number system
Know what each digit in a two-digit number represents.

Instruction
Find a page in a book where 5 is a tens digit. Write down the number and three of the words on the page.

Back in school
The children share their numbers – write them all on the board in order from smallest to largest. What words did they write? What is the longest word?

Objective

Numbers and the number system
Begin to find one half and one quarter of small numbers of objects.

Instruction
Count the number of spoons you have. Now find half that number if you can. It may not be possible without chopping a spoon in half! Write down the number of spoons and bring it into school.

Back in school
Discuss which numbers can be halved and which numbers cannot. Write the numbers which can be halved in one set, and the others in another set.

Look at those which can be halved. Find half and write it down for each number. Can these numbers be halved again?

· · · · · · · ·

Calculations

$$1 + 2 = ?$$

Objective
Calculations
Begin to add 3 digits mentally.

Instruction
Find and write down two car number plates where the digits total less than 12. Draw the best car!

Can be repeated with less/more than 12.

Back in school
Write as many different additions with a total of 10 as you can find.

Objective
Calculations
Know by heart all pairs of numbers with a total of 10/20.

Instruction
Write down the ages of three children you know (try to think of children with different ages e.g. brothers and sisters, cousins etc). Work out how long it will be before they are 10/20.

Back in school
How long it will be before each child in the class is 20? How long before they are 30?

. . . .

Objective
Calculations
Know by heart all pairs of numbers with a total of 20.

Instruction
Write down all the pairs of numbers you know that total 20.

Back in school
Children work in pairs to write three numbers which make 20.

. . . .

Objective
Calculations
Know by heart all pairs of multiples of 10 with a total of 100.

Instruction
Write down all the pairs of multiples of 10 with a total of 100 e.g. 90 + 10.

Back in school
Children work in pairs to write three multiples of 10 which total 100.

. . . .

Objective
Calculations
Use the + and = sign to record mental additions and recognise the use of a symbol such as ? to stand for an unknown number.

Instruction
Add your house number to your age. Then write what you have done as a sum using + and = sign.

Do the same with someone else's house number (perhaps you could ask someone at home for your granny's or aunty's house number).

Bring your two sums into school.

Back in school
Discuss how can the children work out what the house numbers were (assuming they know the child's age)?
Work through some of the examples the children have brought back.

Teacher's note: this activity will then become a problem-solving activity i.e. ?+ 7 = 92.

. . . .

From Geoff Griffiths

Objective
Calculations
Use knowledge that addition can be done in any order to do mental calculations more efficiently. For example: put the larger number first and/or finding pairs totalling 10.

Instructions
Work out the total of the digits of your phone number or the school's phone number. See how good someone at home is at adding them up whilst you say the digits slowly.

Back in school
Play the same game next day in class with each child in turn saying their phone number for a group (or the class) to total. They can write the numbers down before working out the total.

. . . .

Objective
Calculations
Find a small difference by counting up from the smaller to the larger number.

Instruction
Write down your name (first name and surname). Ask someone else in your house to write down their name. Count the number of letters in your name and write the number. Do the same for their name. Work out whose name is the longest and by how many letters.

Back in school
Children work in pairs to work out the difference between the number of letters in their name and their friends.

. . . .

Objective
Calculations
State the subtraction corresponding to a given addition.

Instruction
Find someone to work with. Ask them to write an addition, e.g. 8 + 4 = 12. You have to write a subtraction using the same numbers, e.g. you could write 12 – 4 = 8. Repeat the process the other way around. Bring your additions and subtractions into school.

Back in school
Children work in pairs to write three additions and three corresponding subtractions each.

. . . .

From St. Peter's CE School, Harborne

Objective
Calculations
Know the facts for the 2 and 10 times table.

Instruction
See how quickly you can say your 2 (10) times table backwards! Try it out on an adult and get them to tell you if they think you took less than one minute. See if they can do it faster than you! (You could use a watch that shows seconds to be really accurate.)

Back in school
Time each other in class.
How quickly can the whole class do it?

. . . .

Objective
Calculations
Know by heart doubles for all numbers to 10 and the corresponding halves.

Instruction
Find someone to play with. Sit back to back. You write down a number between 1 and 10. Don't show your partner! Double the number in your head and say the total to the other person, e.g. if you write down 5, you say 10. They have to halve the number you say and tell you their answer. It should be the same as the number you have written down! Now let them have a turn at starting. Play several times.

Back in school
Repeat this game in class, letting the children play in pairs.
How quickly can the whole class do it?

. . . .

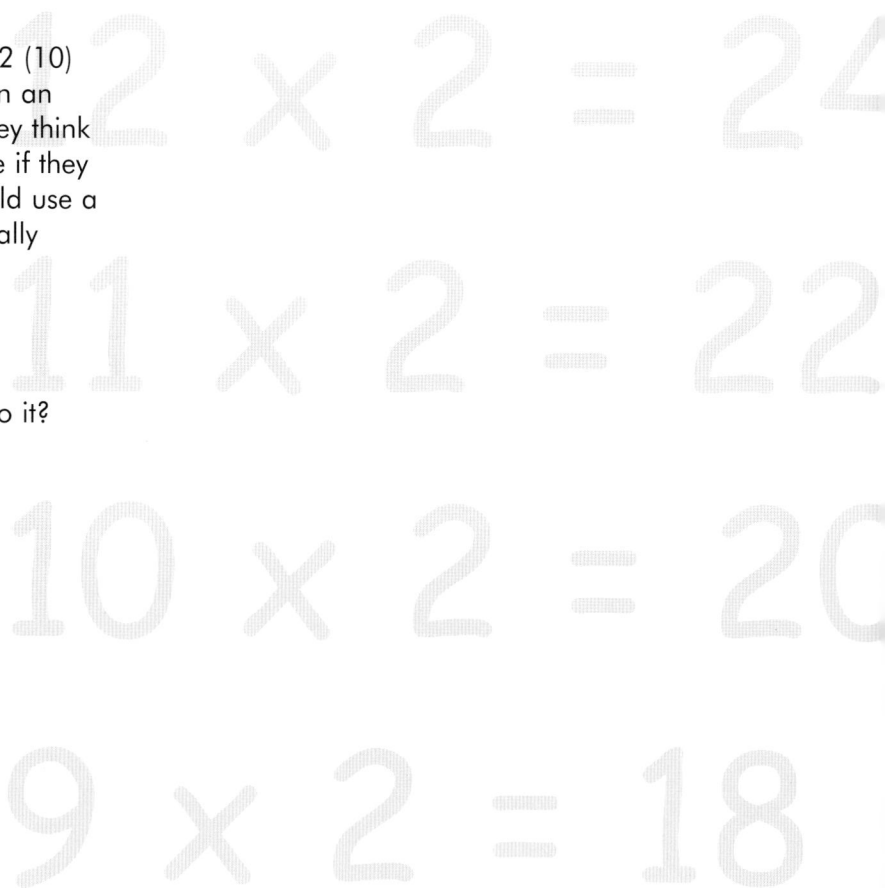

Y2

Solving problems

$$1 + 2 = ?$$

From St. Peter's CE School, Harborne

Objective
Solving problems
Recognise coins and notes of different values.

Instruction
Investigate how many different ways you can make 15p. You can draw around the coins or write down the coins you used. Bring your work to school to show how many ways you have found.

Back in school
Collect as many different ways as you can. How can you be sure you have them all?

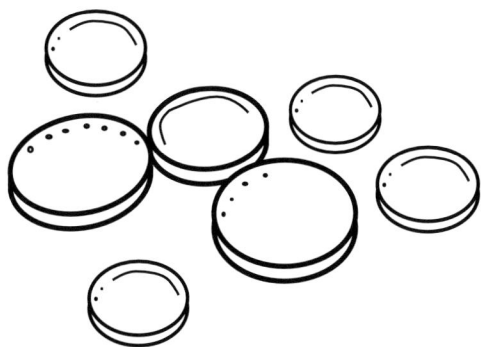

Objective
Solving problems
Recognise coins of different values.

Instruction
Get three coins and write down on a piece of paper how much they are worth altogether. Bring it to school tomorrow.

Back in school
The class have to guess which coins they were as part of the mental/oral session or as part of a maths challenge board.

. . . .

Objective
Solving problems
Recognise coins of different values.

Instruction
Ask someone at home to choose three coins from their purse, but they mustn't let you see what they are. Ask them to tell you how much the three coins total. You must then guess which coins they have. Then you choose three coins, tell your partner the total and see if they can guess which coins you have.

Back in school
Play the same game in class against the teacher or in pairs.

Solving problems
Begin to use £ and p. notation for money.

Instruction
When you go to the supermarket or shop find something that costs between £1 and £2. Draw it with a price label on it.

Back in school
What is the most expensive item? Which is the cheapest?

Discuss how many pence different items cost and write the labels showing pence e.g. £1.45 = 145p.

Order the prices beginning with the cheapest.

Y2

. . . .

From Adderley School, Birmingham

Solving problems
Begin to use £ and p. notation for money.

Instruction
Find out how much your favourite sweet costs. Draw it and label it using £ and p. notation, e.g. £0.37

Back in school
In pairs children work out how much change they would get from £1 if they bought that sweet.

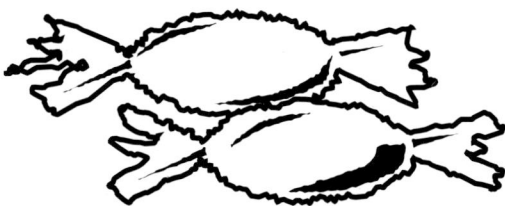

Solving problems
Solve simple word problems involving money.

Instruction
Write down how much pocket money you get this week. Then write down everything you buy and how much it cost. At the end of the week you need to work out how much money you have left – if anything!

Back in school
Compare all the different objects the children think you can buy which cost about 50p.

. . . .

Measures, shape and space

From Adderley School, Birmingham

Objective

Measures, shape and space
Estimate and measure lengths.

Instruction
Find a leaf that is about 10 centimetres long (not counting the stalk). Bring it into school.

Back in school
What other things can you find in class which are about 10 centimetres long? Make a book of 10 centimetres long objects.

. . . .

Objective

Measures, shape and space
Estimate, measure and compare measures using length.

Instruction
Find three things in your home that measure more/less than 1 metre. Draw them, write them down or bring them in.

Back in school
Which are the longest? Which are the shortest?
Choose one object and measure it.

From Anne Bright, Osborne JI School

Objective

Measures, shape and space
Measure length.

Instruction
Give each child a piece of string or wool one metre long. Ask them to find some things at home that are about one metre long or high. Draw these things.

Teacher's note: this can be repeated for different lengths.

Back in school
Compare objects. Estimate another dimension, e.g. depth of the object.

. . . .

Objective

Measures, shape and space
Read and interpret number scales with accuracy.

Instruction
Measure how tall you are.

Back in school
Compare heights. What units did the children use?

Objective

Measures, shape and space

Estimate, measure and compare measures using kilograms.

Instruction

Find three things in your home that each weigh more than 1 kilogram/ less than 1 kilogram. Draw them, write them down or bring them in.

Back in school

Which ones weigh the most? Which weigh the least? Compare using scales.

Y2

. . . .

Objective

Measures, shape and space

Estimate and measure weight.

Instruction

Find a stone that weighs about 50/100 grams. Bring it to school.

Back in school

What things can you find in school that weigh about 50/100 grams? Make a book of objects and drawings of things that weigh about 50/100 grams.

. . . .

Objective

Measures, shape and space

Estimate, measure and compare measures using capacity.

Instruction

Find three things in your home that each hold more/less than 1 litre. Draw them, write them down or bring them in.

Back in school

Which one holds the most? Which holds the least?

. . . .

Objective

Measures, shape and space

Order the months of the year.

Instruction

Find out the birth months of everyone in your house. Put them down in the order that they occur in the year.

Back in school

Make a graph of all the birthdays.

. . . .

From Adderley School, Birmingham

Objective

Measures, shape and space

Understand and use the vocabulary related to time.

Instruction

Where can you find digital time? Look in your house and in the environment. Bring examples into school where you can, e.g. bus tickets, timetables, TV times, etc.

Back in school

Discuss the 24 hour clock.

. . . .

Objective

Measures, shape and space

Know and use the units of time and the relationship between them.

Instruction

Choose two TV programmes. Draw an analogue and digital clock face to show what time they start.

Back in school

Compare times. Which is the earliest programme to start? Which is the latest?

. . . .

From Paul Tremere

Objective

Measures, shape and space

Solve problems involving time and explain how the problem was solved.

Instruction

Write down what time you go to bed tonight. Then write down what time you get up. Work out how long you spent in bed.

Back in school

Work out how many children go to bed before 8 o'clock? How many get up before 7 o'clock?

. . . .

Objective

Measures, shape and space

Make and describe shapes.

Instruction

Find a shape at home that you can draw and then write a few sentences about. Bring your drawing and description to school.

Back in school

Children read their descriptions to one another to see if they can guess what has been drawn.

. . . .

Objective

Measures, shape and space

Begin to recognise line symmetry.

Instruction

Look for some badges or logos that are symmetrical. Car badges are often symmetrical. Look through old magazines or newspapers to see if you can find some. Bring them into school.

Back in school

Look at the logos together. Do any have rotational symmetry? Copy the best examples of symmetry and display them.

. . . .

Objective

Measures, shape and space

Make and describe patterns and begin to recognise line symmetry.

Instruction

Find something at home that you can draw around to make a pattern or picture. Make your picture or pattern with a line of symmetry.

Mark in your line of symmetry. Think about how you can describe your pattern or picture to your friend.

Back in school

Ask some children to describe their pattern to the class, without the class seeing it, and see if they can draw it.

YEAR 3
Numbers and the number system

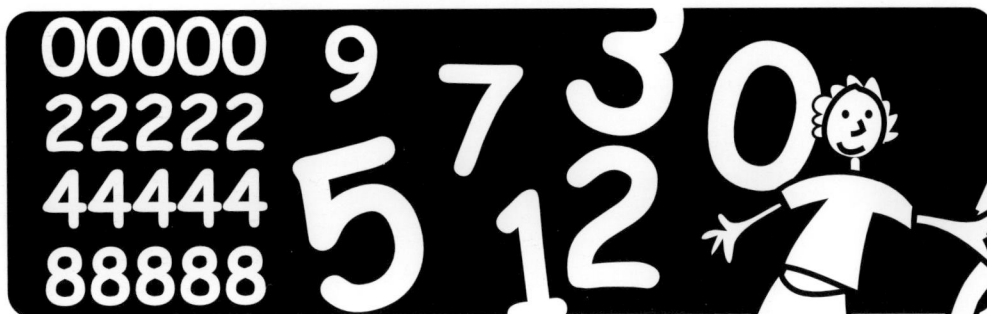

Objective
Numbers and the number system
Count on or back in tens or hundreds, starting from any two- or three-digit number.

Instruction
Draw a blank number line. Write your house number at the beginning of it. Then add 100 to that number and mark it on your number line, do it again and again until you get to more than 1000. How many jumps of a 100 did you make before you got to more than 1000?

Back in school
Work in pairs. Make a number line for each other and jump in 50's.

. . . .

Objective
Numbers and the number system
Recognise two-digit and three-digit multiples of 2, 5 or 10.

Instruction
Look for car number plates which show a number that is a multiple of 2, 5 or 10. Can you find three of one sort?

Back in school
Discuss whether there were any numbers they found that were good for all three numbers and why that is so.

. . . .

Objective
Numbers and the number system
Count on or back in tens or hundreds, starting from any two- or three-digit number.

Instruction
Draw a blank number line, then put 10 marks on there (try to space them evenly). Imagine your house number written at the beginning of it (but don't write it on there!). Now count in 10's up to the end of the number line and write the number that you get to right at the end of it, i.e. start at 132, write at the end of the line 222.

Back in school
Work in pairs so that your friend can fill in the empty spaces by counting back.

Teacher's note: this activity can be adapted for counting in steps of different sizes.

. . . .

Objective

Numbers and the number system
Read whole numbers to at least 1000.

Instruction
On your way home look at the car number plates. Find a number as close to 500 as you can. Jot down your number on a piece of paper. Can you work out how far away from 500 it is? Draw the car.

Back in school
Compare the different numbers. How many were more than 500? How many were less?

S714 AOG

G309 ELR

. . . .

Objective

Numbers and the number system
Know what each digit in a three-digit number represents.

Instruction
Take the last three digits of your phone number (or a friend's) and rearrange them to make the:

      largest number you can
      smallest number you can
      number nearest 500
      largest odd number
      smallest even number, etc.

Back in school
What was the largest number made? What was the smallest? etc.

. . . .

Objective

Numbers and the number system
Round any two-digit number to the nearest ten and any three-digit number to the nearest 100.

Instruction
Look for five car number plates. Write them down and then write the number rounded to the nearest 100.

Back in school
Round each number to the nearest ten. Are any numbers the same when rounded to the nearest ten as they were when rounded to the nearest 100?

. . . .

Objective

Numbers and the number system
Recognise unit fractions such as $1/2$, $1/4$.

Instruction
Get a sheet of newspaper. Fold it in half, and then fold it in half again. Keep going. What is the smallest fraction you can fold it into? Bring it into school.

Back in school
Admire their work! Try the same with an A4 piece of paper.
What do you find?

. . . .

Calculations

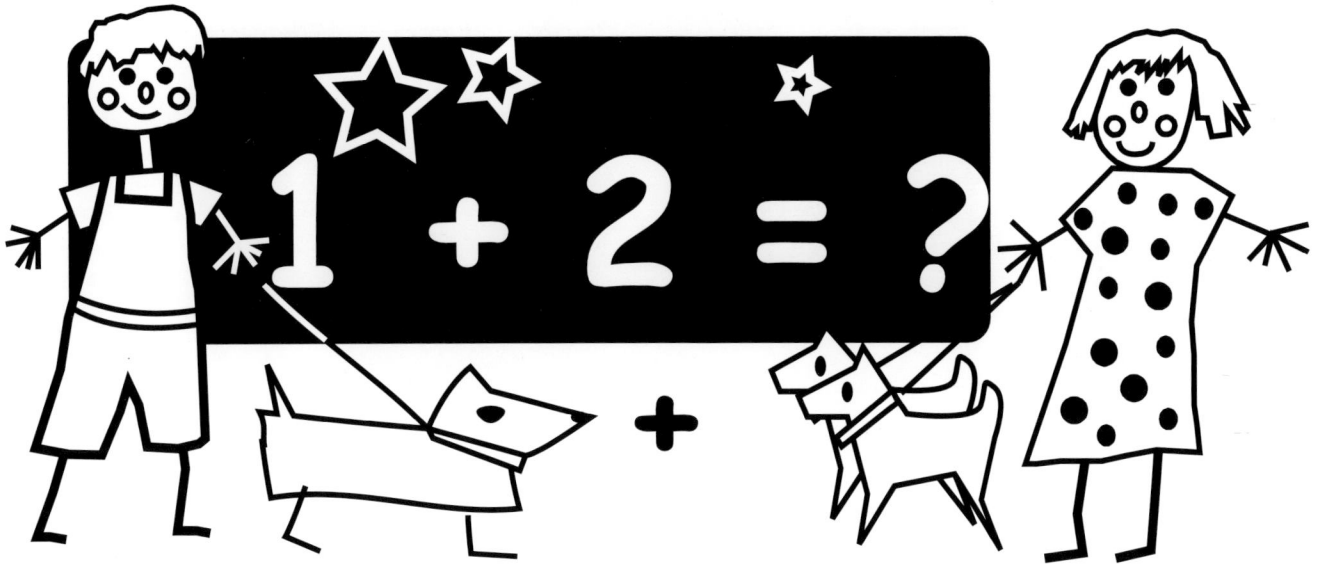

◖Objective◗
Calculations

Add three or four single digit numbers mentally.

Instruction
Write down your phone number or the school's phone number, including the area code. Choosing just four digits try to make a total of 20. If that is not possible get as near to 20 as you can. (It can be over or under.)

Back in school
Compare the children's totals and the number and operations they chose.

. . . .

◖Objective◗
Calculations

Understand that subtraction is the inverse of addition.

Instruction
Make up three 'I'm thinking of a number' problems using addition and subtraction, e.g. I'm thinking of a number. When I add 27 to it I get 53. What is the number? (26)

Back in school
The children work in pairs to try out their puzzles.

◖Objective◗
Calculations

Add two two-digit numbers by partitioning into tens and units then recombining. Explain methods orally (and in writing).

Instruction
Ask someone at home to give you two numbers between one and nine. Make a two-digit number from them. Then reverse the digits to make another two-digit number. Add them together. Then ask them to give you two more numbers and do the same. What do you notice? Why do you think that happens?

Back in school
In pairs discuss your results.
Discuss which numbers lead to a multiple of 11 and which do not (e.g. 87)

. . . .

Objective
Calculations

Find a small difference between (subtract) two numbers by counting on.

Instruction

Ask someone at home to give you two numbers between one and nine. Make them into two two-digit numbers. Find the difference between the two numbers. How did you do it? Explain to your partner.

Back in school

Play this, teacher against class. Who is faster?

. . . .

Objective
Calculations

Use informal pencil and paper methods to support, record, or explain addition/ subtraction.

Instruction

Ask a grown-up you know to calculate 54 + 29 in their head. They may not write any numbers down!

Find out what method of addition they used. Is it the same as yours? If not, show them your method.

Back in school

Practise adding near multiples of ten by adding multiples of ten.

. . . .

Objective
Calculations

Use informal pencil and paper methods to support, record, or explain subtraction.

Instruction

Ask a grown-up you know to calculate 100 – 68 in their head. They may not write any numbers down!

Find out what method of subtraction they used. Is it the same as yours? If not, show them your method.

Back in school

Practise subtracting by counting on.

. . . .

From St. Peter's CE School, Harborne, Birmingham

Objective
Calculations

Begin to know the 3 and 4 times table.

Instruction

See how quickly you can say your 3 (4) times table backwards! Try it out on an adult and get them to tell you if they think you took less than one minute. See if they can do it faster than you can!

Back in school

Time yourselves as a whole class!

. . . .

Objective
Calculations

Derive quickly division/multiplication facts corresponding to the 2, 5 and 10 times table.

Instruction

Ask someone at home to write down a number fact e.g. 5 x 8 = 40

Then write down all the other facts you can derive because you know that

e.g.　40 ÷ 5 = 8
　　　40 ÷ 8 = 5
　　　8 x 5 = 40

Back in school

Write one division fact and ask the children to generate a multiplication fact from it.

. . . .

Objective
Calculations

To multiply by 10/100 shift the digits one/two places to the left.

Instruction

Continue from above e.g. the known fact 5 x 8 = 40. Write down all you can derive because of knowing that,

e.g.　50 x 8 = 400
　　　5 x 80 = 400
　　　400 ÷ 8 = 50
　　　400 ÷ 50 = 8
　　　500 x 8 = 4000
　　　800 x 5 = 4000
　　　4000 ÷ 5 = 800
　　　4000 ÷ 8 = 500 etc.

Back in school

Write one division fact and ask the children to generate a multiplication fact from it.

. . . .

Solving problems

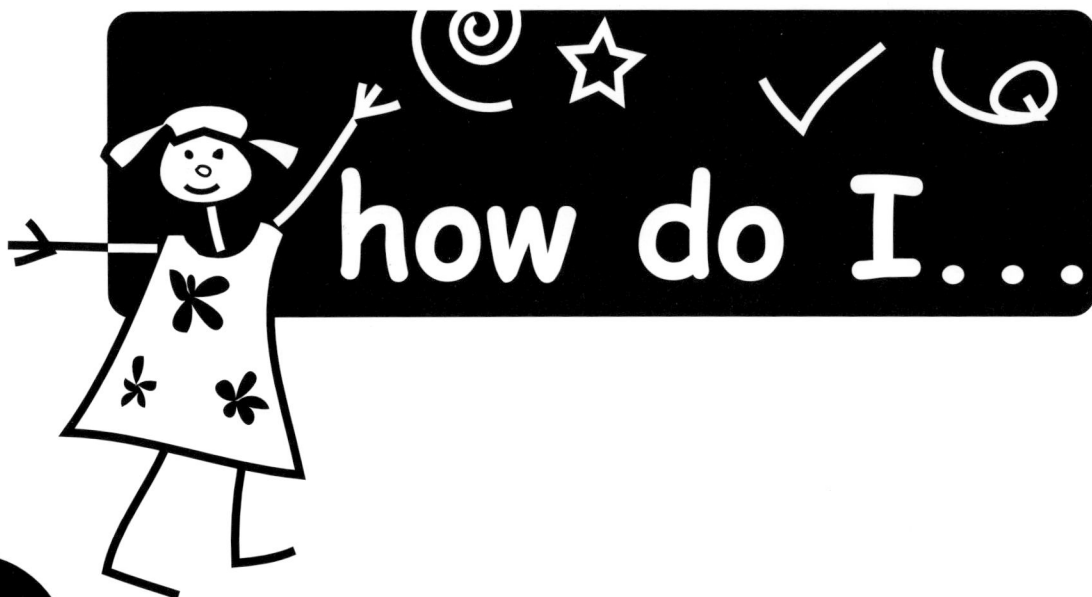

how do I...

Y3

Objective
Solving problems
Choose and use appropriate operations (including multiplication) to solve problems and appropriate ways of calculating, mental, mental with jottings, pencil and paper.

Instruction
Find out the price of a first class stamp and a second class stamp. Work out the cost of two first class stamps. Also two second class stamps. Work out the cost of one first class stamp plus one second class stamp.

Back in school
Explain to your partner how you worked it out.
How many different combinations of first and second class stamps can you buy with a £1 coin?

. . . .

Objective
Solving problems
Recognise coins of different values.

Instruction
Get five coins and write down on a piece of paper how much they are worth altogether. Bring your work to school tomorrow.

Back in school
The class will then have to guess which coins they were as part of the mental/oral session or as part of a maths challenge board.

. . . .

Objective
Solving problems
Recognise coins of different values.

Instruction
Ask someone else to choose five coins from their purse, but they mustn't let you see what they are. Ask them to tell you how much the five coins total. You must then guess which coins they have. Then see if you can do the same for them.

Back in school
Play this, teacher against the class. The teacher chooses five coins and says how much they total. The children guess which coins they are.

. . . .

Objective
Solving problems
Understand and use the £ and p. notation.

Instruction
Find out how much your favourite comic or magazine costs. Then find out the price of the cheapest comic or magazine you can see. Work out the difference in price.

Back in school
Work out approximately the total amount the class spends on comics or magazines in a week!

. . . .

From Adderley School, Birmingham

Objective
Solving problems
Solve simple word problems involving money.

Instruction
Write down how much pocket money you get this week. Then write down everything you buy and how much it cost. At the end of the week you need to work out how much money you have left – if anything!

Back in school
Make a list of all the different objects you can think of which cost about one pound.

. . . .

Handling data

From Anne Bright, Osborne JI School, Birmingham

Objective
Handling data
Organise numerical data in simple tables.

Instruction
Look for something in your house to tally, e.g. the number of Lego bricks you have. Do a tally and bring it to school.

Back in school
Compare the different objects counted!

. . . .

Measures, shape and space

From Anne Bright, Osborne JI School, Birmingham

Objective
Measures, shape and space
Measure length (of objects that are not straight).

Instruction
Give the children a piece of string or wool one metre long. Show them how to use it to measure things that are not straight, e.g. the circumference of the top of a waste bin. Ask the children to use their string to find things that are about one metre around or along.

Back in school
Compare the different things they found with a circumference of one metre.

On another night give them a piece of paper and ask them to make a 'one metre string-picture', by sticking their string to the paper using sticky tape. They can be as creative as they please. They can stick it more permanently and artistically (!) with glue at school.

. . . .

From Adderley School, Birmingham

Objective
Measures, shape and space
Use units of time (seconds).

Instruction
Find a watch that enables you to count seconds. Time some adverts on the television. Write down which is the longest and which the shortest.

If you haven't got a watch that you can use, count the number of seconds. Teach the children how to count seconds by saying one second, two seconds, three seconds, etc. This should take about three seconds to say. Or one elephant, two elephants, three elephants... etc.

Back in school
Make a graph of advert lengths, ranges 0 – 60 seconds, 60 – 120 seconds, 120 – 180 seconds.

. . . .

From Linda Surga, Hollyfield JI School, Birmingham

Objective
Measures, shape and space
Use units of time and know the relationship between them.

Instruction
Think of an activity that you do outside school that takes about:

   1 minute
   5 minutes
   1 hour, etc.

Write down these activities.

Teacher's note: this activity can obviously be done in different years and with different lengths of times.

Back in school
Compare all the different activities. Did any children put the same activity, e.g. cleaning your teeth, with different times?

Objective
Measures, shape and space
Use units of time and know the relationship between them.

Instruction
Look in the paper and work out the length of three TV programmes you like to watch.

Back in school
Children work in pairs to calculate the time they would spend watching TV if they watched all three programmes.

. . . .

Objective
Measures, shape and space
Make and describe shapes.

Instruction
Find an object at home that you can draw and then write a few sentences about. Make sure that you use mathematical language wherever you can. Use the language of shape and write down the length, width and perhaps weight of the object too. You can describe what it is made of, if that is helpful, but try to leave that until last.

Teachers note: encourage the children to describe household objects. You might need to give them some examples of descriptions first.

Back in school
Bring your drawings and description to school so that you can read your description to your friend and they see if they can guess what it is you have drawn.

. . . .

Measures, shape and space
Identify lines of symmetry in simple shapes.

Instruction
Look for something in your house that has a line of symmetry. Sketch it and mark in the line of symmetry.

Back in school
Compare the objects and drawings. Did many children choose the same object? Did they always find the same line of symmetry?

. . . .

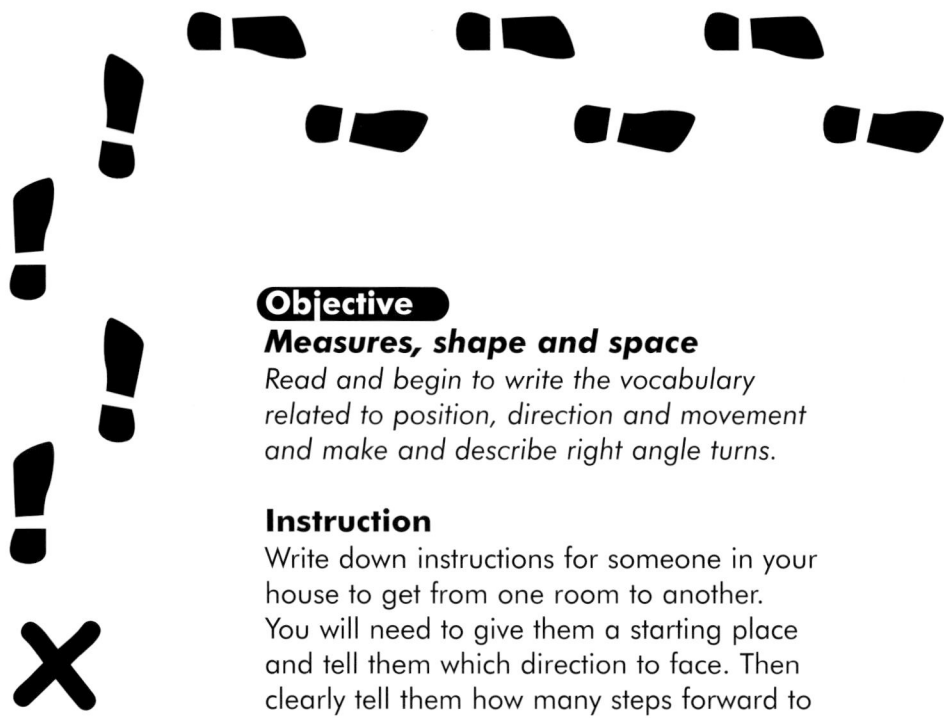

Objective

Measures, shape and space
Read and begin to write the vocabulary related to position, direction and movement and make and describe right angle turns.

Instruction
Write down instructions for someone in your house to get from one room to another. You will need to give them a starting place and tell them which direction to face. Then clearly tell them how many steps forward to take, which way to turn (in quarter turns) and so on. Do not make it too complicated – about six instructions should be enough. When you have tried it out on someone, ask them if they thought the instructions were good enough for them to have done it blindfolded! Report back to your teacher about what they said!

Back in school
Discuss how you instructed the person! How many right angle turns make a circle?

. . . .

Y3

YEAR 4
Numbers and the number system

From Jackie Hughes, Trescott JI School

Objective

Numbers and the number system

Partition numbers into thousands, hundreds, tens and units.
Read and write whole numbers to at least 10,000 in figures and words.

Instruction

Take the last four digits of your phone number (or the school's phone number) and make the:

> largest number you can
> smallest number you can
> number nearest 5000
> largest odd number
> smallest even number, etc.

Back in school

Compare numbers in one of these categories. Whose is the largest? The smallest? The nearest to 5000? etc.

Objective

Numbers and the number system, Solving problems

Recognise the outcomes of sums or differences of pairs of odd/even numbers.

Instruction

Write down this problem for someone in your home.
Can they work out what it means?

> E + E = E
> O + O = E
> O + E = O

Teacher's note: make sure the children know that E = even number, O = odd number. You could ask the children to think of examples to prove it.

The next time (or as well): can they make up the rule for subtraction?

Back in school

What are the rules for multiplication?

From Barbara Teffer, Highfield JI School, Birmingham.

Objective
Numbers and the number system
Recognise multiples of 2, 3, 4, 5 and 10 up to the tenth multiple.

Instruction
Make your own multiple flowers or multiple rockets.

Back in school
Display the best examples.

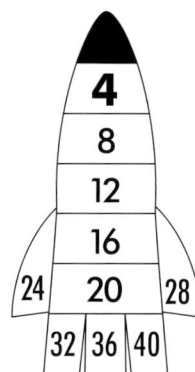

Calculations

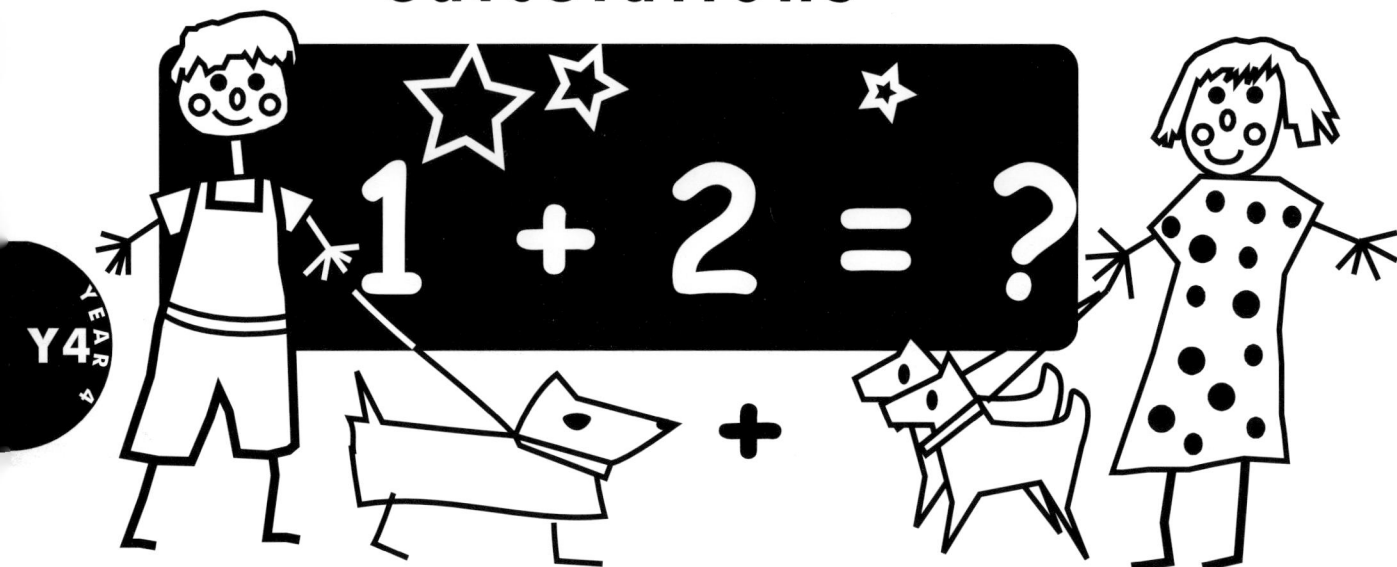

Y4

1 + 2 = ?

Objective
Calculations
Use the relationship between addition and subtraction to solve problems.

Instruction
Make up a puzzle, e.g. I'm thinking of a number; when I add 12 to it I get 35. Ask someone in your home, 'What was the number?' (23).

(Note: this is the same idea as ☐ + 12 = 35.)
They can make up a puzzle for you. Write down your two puzzles and bring them into school.

Back in school
Try out your puzzles on each other, working in pairs.

Objective
Calculations
Derive quickly all pairs of numbers that total 100.

Instruction
Write down the ages of three adults you know. Work out how long it will be before they get a telegram from the Queen (King?) for their hundredth birthday!

Back in school
Work out exactly how long before each of the children gets a telegram to the nearest month! How about if there was a telegram at 50?

. . . .

Objective
Calculations

Use informal pencil and paper methods to support, record or explain mental additions.

Instruction

Write down a code where each letter of the alphabet is worth a number. Use the code A = 1, B = 2 etc. Now work out the total value of your first name.

Back in school

Use this the basis for a handling data exercise, using ranges of numbers if appropriate e.g. value 1–10, 11–20 etc.

. . . .

Objective
Calculations

Begin to know multiplication facts for the 8 times table.

Instruction

Show a grown-up you know how you can work out the 8 times table by doubling the 4 times table.

Back in school

Work out the 6 times table by doubling the 3 times table, and the 12 times table by doubling the 6 times table.

. . . .

Objective
Calculations

Begin to know multiplication facts for the 9 times table.

Instruction

Teach a grown-up you know to use their fingers to work out the 9 times table. Tell your teacher how good they were at learning the method and how fast they were at working out the answers!

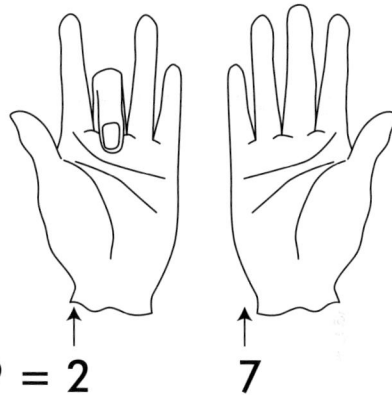

$3 \times 9 = 2 \qquad 7$

Back in School

Try out other finger methods for learning our tables.

. . . .

Objective
Calculations

Use doubling, starting from known facts.

Instruction

Write down any number below 10. Keep doubling it. How far can you go? Which two starting numbers bring you closest to 100 by doubling? (3 i.e. 3 → 6 → 12 → 24 → 48 → 96)

Back in school

Try trebling some different starting numbers which brings you closest to 100?

. . . .

Calculations

Use the relationship between multiplication and division.

Instruction

Ask someone at home to write down a number fact e.g. $12 \times 6 = 72$.

Then write down all the other facts you can derive because you know that, e.g.

$$72 \div 6 = 12$$
$$72 \div 12 = 6$$
$$6 \times 12 = 72$$
$$11 \times 6 = 66$$
$$13 \times 6 = 78, \text{ etc.}$$

Back in school

Write one division fact and ask the children to generate a multiplication fact from it.

. . . .

Objective

Calculations

Use known number facts and place value to multiply or divide mentally.

Instruction

Ask someone at home to give you a fact from a times table e.g. $9 \times 5 = 45$. Write down all you can derive because of knowing that, e.g.

$$90 \times 5 = 450$$
$$9 \times 50 = 450$$
$$450 \div 5 = 90$$
$$450 \div 9 = 50$$
$$900 \times 5 = 4500$$
$$9 \times 500 = 4500$$
$$4500 \div 9 = 500$$
$$4500 \div 5 = 900$$
$$90 \times 50 = 4500, \text{ etc.}$$

Back in school

Write one division fact and ask the children to generate a multiplication fact from it.

. . . .

Y4

Objective

Calculations

Approximate first. Use informal pencil and paper methods to support, record or explain multiplication.

Instruction

Work out how many complete months you have been alive.

Back in school

Compare the numbers of months. The children work in pairs to calculate how many months they have to go until the next multiple of 100!

Solving problems

how do I...

Objective
Solving problems

Choose and use appropriate number operations and appropriate ways of calculating.
Use the vocabulary related to time.

Instruction
Do you think you have been alive for more or less than 500 weeks? Work it out.

Back in school
Can you find out how many days you have lived?

Objective
Solving problems

Solve mathematical problems or puzzles. Use the language of multiplication and addition.

Instruction
Work with someone at home to make up five puzzles for the class to solve in a mental/oral session using the words 'sum' and 'product', e.g. which pair of numbers have a sum of 7 and a product of 12?

Back in school
Work in groups of four to solve each other's puzzles.

Objective
Solving problems

Solve simple word problems involving money.

Instruction

Imagine you have £20 to spend. Write a list of the things you would buy and their exact cost. (You might want to look in local papers, catalogues or shops.) How much would you have left?

Back in school

Collect the children's purchases in categories, e.g. electrical goods, and work out the total cost of each category.

· · · · · · · ·

Objective
Solving problems

Solve money problems using one or more steps.

Instruction

Ask your mum or carer for a till receipt with more than five items on it. Write down the cost of the two cheapest items and add them together. Then do the same for the two most expensive items. Then work out the difference between the two totals!

Back in school

Compare prices, totals, and differences. It is best if children work in groups of four to do this.

· · · · · · · ·

Objective
Solving problems

Use all four operations to solve word problems involving measure (weight).

Instruction

Find/collect some different food labels in your cupboard at home. Then make up two different measuring problems for your friend to solve.

Teacher's note: this can be adjusted so that you tell the children how many steps you want their problems to be. This would also be good for differentiation.

Back in school

The children work in pairs and solve each other's problems.

· · · · · · · ·

From Adderley School, Birmingham

Objective
Solving problems

Solve problems involving time and explain how the problem was solved.

Instruction

Write down what time you go to bed tonight. Then write down what time you get up. Work out how long you spent in bed. Do that for every night this week. At the end of the week work out how long you have spent in bed!

Back in school

Put all the data you have collected about how long you spent in bed this week into a graph. Can you think of some questions to ask your classmates about the graph you have produced?

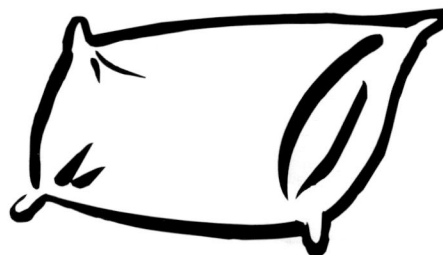

Y4

Objective

Solving problems

Use all four operations to solve word problems involving time.

Instruction

Starting from now, keep a time diary of your next 24 hours (or of your weekend, etc). Bring it to school because you are going to make up some time problems for others in the class to solve, e.g. how long did I spend in bed between midnight on Friday and midnight on Saturday?

Teacher's note: how precise you want the children to be will depend on their ability.

Back in school

Work in groups of four to solve each others' problems.

Handling data

From Adderley School, Birmingham

Objective

Handling data

Organise data in Venn diagrams.

Instruction

Find things in the house that use mains electricity or batteries. Which can run off either? Put this into a Venn diagram.

Back in school

Combine all their information onto a class Venn diagram.

Y4

Measures, shape and space

From St. Peter's CE School, Harborne

Objective
Measures, shape and space
Suggest suitable units to estimate or measure length.

Instruction
Suggest what you might measure using kilometres, metres, centimetres, millimetres.

Back in school
Write one suggestion for each unit. Collect the children's ideas. Give an estimate for the length of several suggestions.

Objective
Measures, shape and space
Suggest suitable units to estimate and measure length.
Explain reasoning when solving a problem.

Instruction
Count the number of strides between two places in your home, e.g. your bedroom door to the front door, or your front door to the garden, etc. Then estimate what that is in metres. Think about how you got your answer so that you can explain it to the class or a friend.

Teacher's note: this activity is more about approximation than exact measure, i.e. 10 strides is probably about 7 – 8 metres.

Back in school
Use the skills of approximating the children practised at home to estimate as accurately as possible the distance from the board to the door (or window to door) in the classroom. Estimate to the nearest 10 cm. Everyone has a guess. Who is closest?

Objective
Measures, shape and space
Know and use the relationship between familiar units of length.
Measure the perimeter of simple shapes.

Instruction
You will need a tape measure or a piece of string and a ruler. Ask someone in your family to lie on the ground with their arms by their sides and their legs together. Using a tape measure or your string measure their perimeter!

Write it down in metres and centimetres and in centimetres.

Teacher's note: if a child hasn't got a ruler they could use a piece of string a metre long, perhaps marked every 10 centimetres.

Back in school
Compare the lengths. Discuss how tall each chosen person was, and the relation of height to perimeter.

. . . .

Objective
Measures, shape and space
Use a.m., p.m. and the notation 9.53.

Instruction
Look at a post box to see what time mail is collected. Find out:
- if there are more collections in the morning or the afternoon
- the time of the latest collection
- if there is a collection everyday

Back in school
Compare collections. Which post box has the latest collection? How much later is it than the next latest?

. . . .

Objective
Measures, shape and space
Describe and visualise 2D and 3D shapes.

Instruction
Find someone at home to be your partner. Fold a piece of A4/A5 paper in half. Decide on a shape (2D or 3D as appropriate). Write three facts about the shape you have chosen on the outside of your paper. Write the name of the mystery shape on the inside fold of your paper.

Your partner has to guess what your shape is from the facts you have given them, so make sure you give them clear information using the correct language.

Back in school
Repeat the exercise, playing the game teacher against the class and having two turns each!

. . . .

Objective
Measures, shape and space
Describe and visualise 3D shapes.

Instruction
Find a shape at home that you can draw and then write a few sentences about. Make sure that you use mathematical language wherever you can. Try to use not only the language of shape but of length, weight etc. Bring your drawing and description to school.

Teacher's note: encourage the children to describe household objects: you might need to give them some examples of descriptions first.

Back in school
The children read descriptions to a friend and they see if the other can guess what it is they have drawn.

. . . .

Measures, shape and space

Begin to know that angles are measured in degrees and estimate angles.

Instruction

Find an example at home or on the way home of:

> an angle of 90°
> an angle of between 90° and 45°
> an angle less than 45°

Make a drawing of the examples you find.

Back in school

Discuss the examples the children have found.
Which were easiest to find?

....

Y4

YEAR 5
Numbers and the number system

Objective
Numbers and the number system
Read and write whole numbers in figures and words, and know what each digit represents.

Instruction
Write your phone number or the school's phone number in words!

Back in school
Discuss and compare numbers. Whose is largest? Whose is smallest? Whose is nearest to one million?

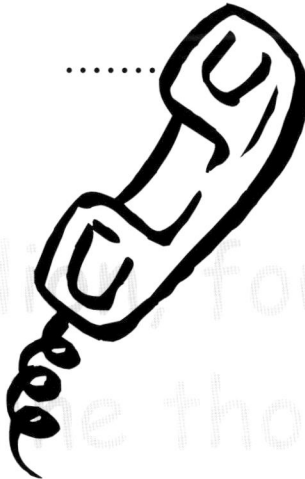

Objective
Numbers and the number system
Read and write whole numbers in figures and in words.

Instruction
Look in your local free paper at the properties for sale adverts. Find a house or flat for sale that costs between £5,000 and £15,000 and one that costs between £15,000 and £50,000.

Teacher's note: these numbers can to be adjusted as appropriate for local conditions.

Back in school
Bring in the adverts and compare your findings.

From Geoff Griffiths

Numbers and the number system

Read and write numbers in figures and in words.
Use informal pencil and paper methods to support, record or explain subtraction calculations.

Instruction

Think about the different ways you can break up your phone number or the school's phone number.

For example, my phone number is 2465152 but I could say it's twenty four, sixty five, one hundred and fifty two.
    OR
two hundred and forty six, five thousand one hundred and fifty two.
    OR
two thousand four hundred and sixty five, one hundred and fifty two

Think about all the different ways you can break up your phone number. Then write them down.

Which do you think is the easiest way to remember your phone number?

Back in school

The children work in groups of four. Take the last four digits of everyone's phone number and work out the differences.

. . . .

Objective

Number and the number system

Use the vocabulary of estimation and approximation. Round any integer up to 10,000 to the nearest 10, 100, 1000.

Instruction

Look in your free paper. Find some prices, for example, of houses or cars which are not in round figures, e.g. £7699. Choose three different cars and round each one to the nearest 10, 100 and 1000. Cut them out and bring them to school.

Back in school

Discuss which cars look good value and which do not. What factors will you need to take into account to make a judgement, e.g. age, mileage, model of car, etc.

. . . .

From Barbara Teffer, Highfield JI School

Objective

Numbers and the number system

Recognise multiples of 6, 7, 8, 9 up to the tenth multiple.

Instruction

Make your own multiple skittles or shirts.

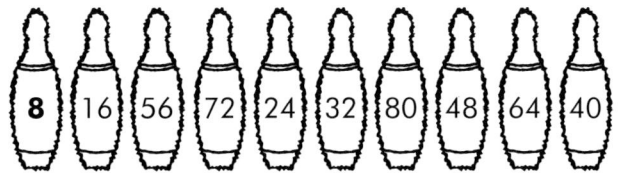

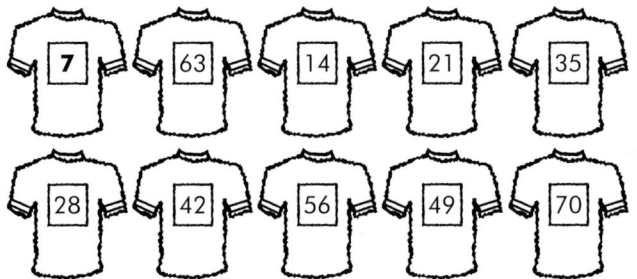

Back in school

Display the best examples that the children bring in.

. . . .

From Barbara Teffer, Highfield JI School

Find all the pairs of factors of any number up to 100.

Instruction
Talk to someone at home about factors. Together find all the pairs of factors for any number up to 100.
Then make your own factor flowers or rockets.

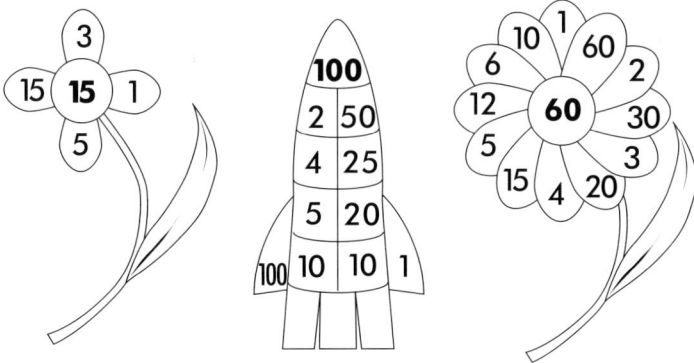

Back in school
Display the best examples of factor flowers or rockets that the children bring in.

. . . .

From Margaret McKeever

Objective
Numbers and the number system
Use fraction notation, including mixed numbers, and the vocabulary numerator and denominator.

Instruction
Work out how old you are in halves! Then work out how old some others in your family are in halves.

Draw pictures of your family and write their ages in halves.

Back in school
Working in pairs and taking turns, one child tells the age, in halves, of someone in their family and the other works out how many whole years old they are.

Objective
Numbers and the number system
Use fraction notation, including mixed numbers, and the vocabulary numerator and denominator.

Instruction
Work out how old you are in quarter years! Then work out how old some others in your family are in quarters.

Draw pictures of your family and write their ages in quarters.

Back in school
Work out how many quarters old the school is!

. . . .

Objective
Numbers and the number system
Order a set of fractions.

Instruction
Take the last three or four digits of your phone number (or the school's phone number). Use the digits to make fractions less than one, e.g. digits 2, 3, 8 will make $2/3$, $2/8$, $3/8$.

There will be three possible fractions if there are three different digits, and six possible combinations if there are four different digits. Sort the fractions into those that are less than one half and those that are more than one half.

Back in school
The children work in groups of four to put all their fractions in order from smallest to largest.

. . . .

Numbers and the number system, Solving problems

Relate fractions to division.
Solve number problems involving money.

Instruction

Look in your local free paper. Find three houses that you would like to buy if money were no object!

Imagine the estate agent was increasing the price of each by a quarter. Cross out the old price and put in the new.

Back in school

Compare the house prices. Which is the most expensive and by how much?

· · · · · · · ·

From Barbara Teffer, Highfield JI School

Objective
Numbers and the number system

Know what each digit represents in a number with up to two decimal places.

Instruction

Look for examples of big numbers (and decimals) for example in the newspapers, reference books, etc. Bring them into school or write down the number and where you saw it.

Back in school

The children can write the number in words. They can try writing the number before and the number after each of their big numbers.

Objective
Numbers and the number system

Round a number with one or two decimal places to the nearest integer.

Instruction

Look in your local free paper and find prices of goods that are advertised. Choose three adverts and round the amount in the advert to the nearest pound.

Back in school

Compare the prices of the goods. Discuss which seem to be good value and which seem to be expensive.

· · · · · · · ·

From Barbara Teffer, Highfield JI School

Objective
Numbers and the numbers system

Begin to understand percentages.

Instruction

Look for examples of percentage symbols in newspapers, signs, etc. Bring some into school, if you can, or note them down.

Back in school

Discuss the different examples brought in and make a display of them.

· · · · · · · ·

Y5

Objective
Numbers and the number system
Find simple percentages of whole numbers.

Instruction
Imagine you are going to buy a car from your local free paper. The owner wants a 10% deposit so that he can tell you are really serious about wanting it, before you raise the rest of the money. Find a car that you might like to buy, cut out the advert and write on it the amount of the deposit you will have to give the owner. Bring the advert to school.

Back in school
Compare the car prices. Discuss how reasonable they seem.

Think about the factors you need to take into account to see if they are good value, e.g. age, mileage, model of car, etc.

FOR SALE

Y5

Calculations

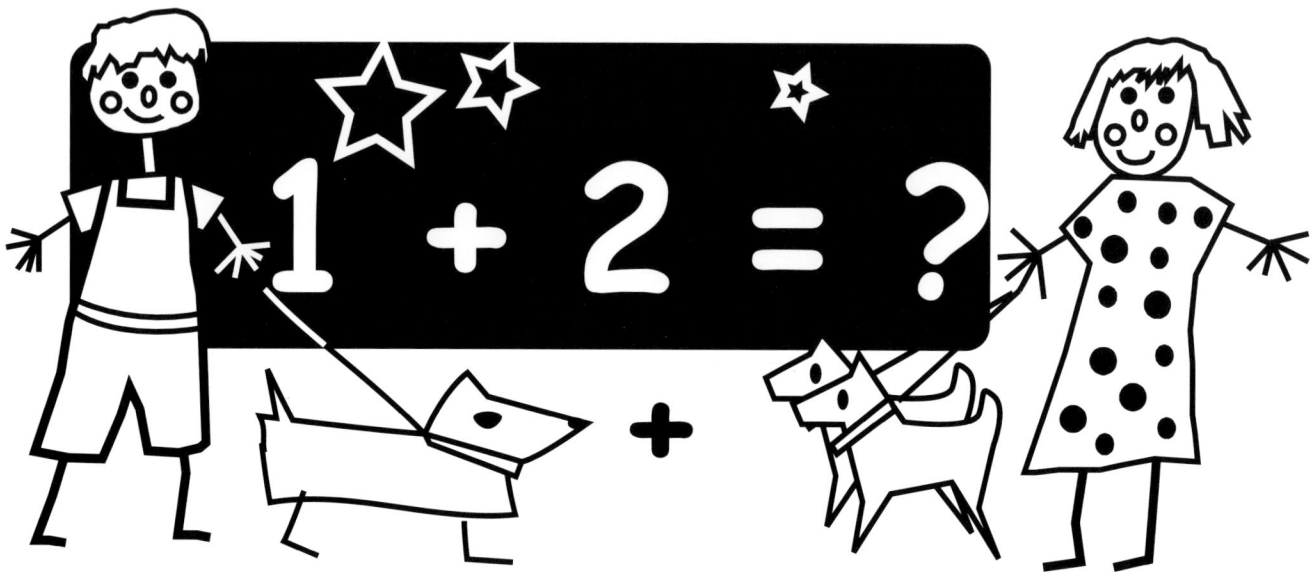

From Barbara Teffer, Highfield JI School

Objective
Calculations

Add several single digit numbers.

Instruction
Make your own consecutive numbers caterpillars.

Y5 YEAR 5

Back in school
Display the best examples that the children bring in.

· · · · · · · ·

Objective
Calculations

Use known number facts and place value for mental addition and subtraction. (Using paper and pencil to support the calculation if necessary.)

Instruction
Ask your mum how old some of your relations are and then work out what year they were born. Tell your mum that she mustn't tell you that before you start! Try working out the birth year of a granny and an aunt or uncle.

Back in school
Whose granny is oldest? Work out how many months your granny has lived.

· · · · · · · ·

Use the relationship between multiplication and division, addition and subtraction to solve problems.

Instruction

Ask someone at home to help you to make up a two-step 'I'm thinking of a number' problem. Use multiplication and division and/or addition and subtraction. E.g. 'I'm thinking of a number; when I double it and then divide by 8, I get 4. What was the number?' (16).

Back in school

Work in pairs (or fours) to solve each other's problems.

· · · · · · · ·

Use the relationship between multiplication and division.
Choose and use appropriate number operations to solve problems and appropriate ways of calculating.

Instruction

Make up two multiplication and two division sums. Then write them out again putting an empty box where one of the numbers should be, e.g.

$13 \times 14 = 182$ ➡ $13 \times \square = 182$
$304 \div 8 = 38$ ➡ $\square \div 8 = 38$

You can make some of them difficult enough to need a calculator if you want or calculations that can be worked out mentally or with paper and pencil.
Bring them back to school for others in your class to work out the missing number.

Back in school

Work in pairs (or fours) to solve each other's problems.

· · · · · · · ·

Solving problems

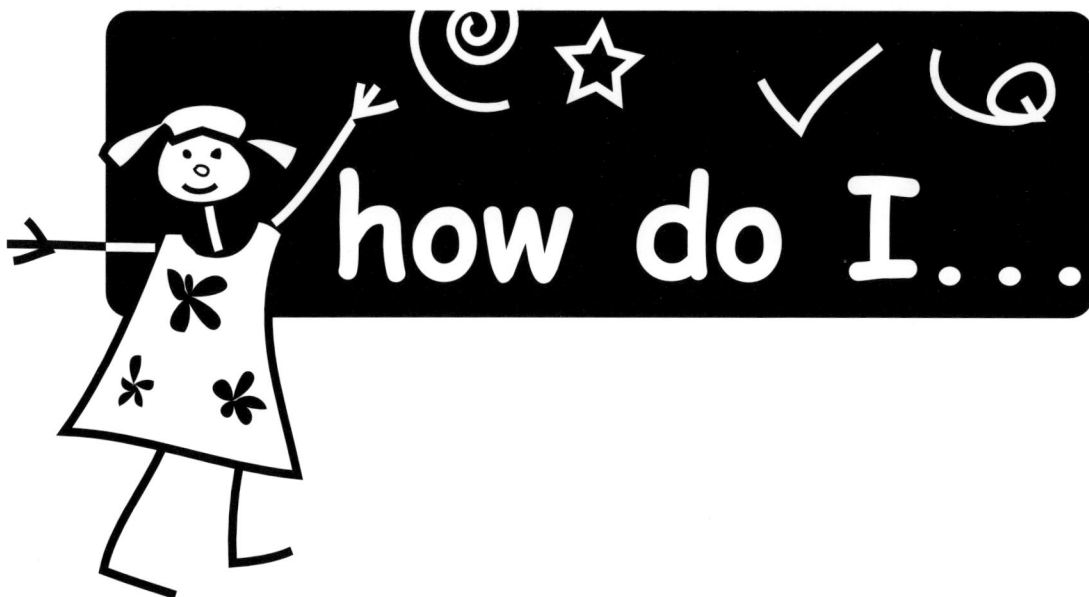

how do I...

Objective
Solving problems

Solve mathematical problems or puzzles, recognise and explain patterns and relationships.

Instruction
Choose two numbers between 1 and 9. Make them into two different two-digit numbers. Find the difference between the two numbers. Ask someone at home to do the same with two different numbers. Then with two more. What do you notice about the differences you get? Why do you think this happens?

Clue: think of one of your multiplication tables.

Back in school
Discuss and try to explain why the differences are in the 9 times table.

. . . .

Objective
Solving problems

Solve mathematical problems or puzzles.

Instruction
Choose any nine consecutive numbers and make up a magic square.

Teacher's note: give an example of a magic square. You may also want to give the children the range of numbers to use, e.g. higher achievers any nine consecutive numbers between 50 and 100, lower achievers between 0 and 12.)

Back in school
The children work in groups of four to check each other's squares. Are they magic? Display those that are.

. . . .

Objective
Solving problems
Solve simple problems involving money.

Instruction
Write down a target of £10. Decide what items you could buy which would total exactly £10. You must choose more than two things. You may want to look in your local paper, catalogues, menus from take-aways, etc, as well as in shops.
Write down the things you would buy and their prices.

Back in school
Compare the different things the children chose to buy which were good value!

. . . .

Objective
Solving problems
Use all four operations to solve simple word problems using money.

Instruction
Look at the small advertisements in the local free paper. Find three things that you could buy if you had £100 to spend. Get as close as you can to £100. Tear the adverts out and bring them to school.

There could be house points or a prize for the children who get closest to £100.

Back in school
Discuss the value of the items chosen. Which ones seem particularly good value? How can you tell? What factors do you take into account?

. . . .

Objective
Solving problems
Solve money problems using one or more steps.

Instruction
Ask your mum or carer for a till receipt with more than five items on it. Write down the cost of the two or three cheapest items and add them together. Then do the same for the two or three most expensive items. Next work out the total cost of the four to six items. Then work out how much change you would get if you paid with a £20 note.

Back in school
Have any of the children chosen the same items? Compare prices.

. . . .

Objective
Solving problems
Use all four operations to solve word problems involving measure (weight, capacity).

Instruction
Find and collect some different food labels in your cupboard at home. Then make up two different measuring problems for your friend to solve.

Can you make up a problem which involves multiplication or division? Can you make up a problem which involves two or three steps to solve it?

Teacher's note: this can be adjusted so that you tell the children how many steps you want their problems to be. This would also good for differentiation.

Back in school
Children work in groups of four to solve each other's problems.

. . . .

Objective
Solving problems
Use all four operations to solve problems involving time.

Instruction
Look in the local free paper and find the advert for the local multi-screen cinema. It gives the start time for all the films. If you have to allow 35 minutes for the cinema to empty and the new audience to take their seats and also for the trailers which advertise coming films, you can work out approximately the length of each film.

Work out which is the longest/shortest film and how long it is, or work out the length of each film.
Bring the advert into school.

Back in school
Discuss and compare film lengths. What is the longest film anyone has seen? What is the shortest?

. . . .

From Barbara Teffer, Highfield JI School

Objective
Solving problems
Use appropriate operations to solve problems using one or more steps (time).

Instruction
Write down all the programmes you watch on television tonight and how long each one lasts.

Back in school
The children work in pairs to find their total viewing time!
Perhaps you can graph the results?

. . . .

Objective
Solving problems
Use all four operations to solve word problems involving time.

Instruction
Keep a time diary of about a six-hour period in any day you choose between now and when the homework has to be returned. Try to make it as precise as you can, e.g. 7.55 a.m. got up; 8.07 a.m. finished washing and dressing, etc.
Bring it to school.

Back in school
The children work in pairs and make up some time problems for their partner to solve. For example: how long did it take me to wash and dress?

Handling data

Objective
Handling data
Discuss the chance or likelihood of particular events.

Instruction
Write a statement for each of these words:
● Certain
● Likely
● Unlikely
● Impossible
Talk to someone at home about what you have written. Do they agree with you?

Back in school
In pairs draw a scale which goes from 'no chance', through 'poor chance', 'even chance' and 'good chance' to 'certain'. Place the statements they have written on the scale in the appropriate positions. Then together think of a statement that would be appropriate for the 'evens chance' position.

Measures, shape and space

From St. Peter's CE School, Harborne

Objective
Measures, shape and space
Suggest suitable units to estimate and measure length.
Understand the relationship between units.

Instruction
Count the number of strides between two places in your home, e.g. your bedroom door to the front door, or your front door to the garden etc. Then estimate what that is in metres and centimetres.

Back in school
This activity can be the start of an exercise in problem-solving which could involve measuring the length of their stride and multiplying it by the number of strides taken. Then compare this with their approximation. It also involves dealing with different units of measure.

. . . .

Objective
Measures, shape and space
Read the time on a 24-hour digital clock.

Instruction
Find the times of your three favourite TV programmes. If you had to programme the video, draw what the display would look like when the programme started. Bring it into school.

Back in school
Look at what the children have brought back. Discuss how easy or difficult they found the task and the advantages and disadvantages of using the 24-hour clock.

Objective
Measures, shape and space
Use units of time; read the time on a 24-hour digital clock and use the 24-hour clock notation, such as 19:53. Use timetables.

Instruction
Find something that shows times using the 24-hour clock. (The local free paper usually shows start times for films using the 24-hour clock if timetables are not available.) Cross out the shown time and convert it to 12-hour times using a.m. or p.m.

Back in school
Play a game: teacher says a time in 12 hours; children have to say the same time using 24-hour clock. Play the other way round as well. Who is quicker?

. . . .

Objective
Measures, shape and space
Complete symmetrical patterns with two lines of symmetry at right angles (using squared paper).

Instruction
Each child will need a piece of squared paper. In school they should draw a vertical line the length of their paper, as near to the middle as they can (so that their drawn line is on a printed line). Then do the same with a horizontal line. The paper should now be in four parts.

At home design a simple pattern using coloured pencils or pens or crosses in squares in one of the four sections. Then reflect that pattern in just one of the other sections. Then bring it to school.

Back in school
The children work in pairs to complete the pattern using reflection in the other two sections.

. . . .

Objective
Measures, shape and space
Recognise where a shape will be after reflection and/or translation.

Instruction
Look for a pattern in your home that uses translation or reflection, e.g. wallpaper, carpets, tiling, packaging. Bring it to school or sketch it.

Back in school
Compare patterns. Did any two children find the same pattern?

. . . .

Objective
Measures, shape and space
Recognise parallel and perpendicular lines in the environment.

Instruction
Look for examples of parallel and perpendicular lines in your home or in the environment. Sketch or write down where you have seen them.

Back in school
Discuss the different examples and try to describe some others (e.g. bridges, towers, etc).

. . . .

From Juliette Blagg, Kings Norton Primary
School

Objective

Measures, shape and space
*Identify and estimate obtuse and acute
angles.*

Instruction
Look around your home and on your
journey to school. See if you can find five
examples of obtuse and acute angles.
Make a mental note of these so you can tell
the class tomorrow.

Back in school
Discuss: did anyone spot the same angles
on objects? Which angles were easiest to
find? Why? Did anyone find a shape or
object that had no angles, or a different
(reflex) angle?

. . . .

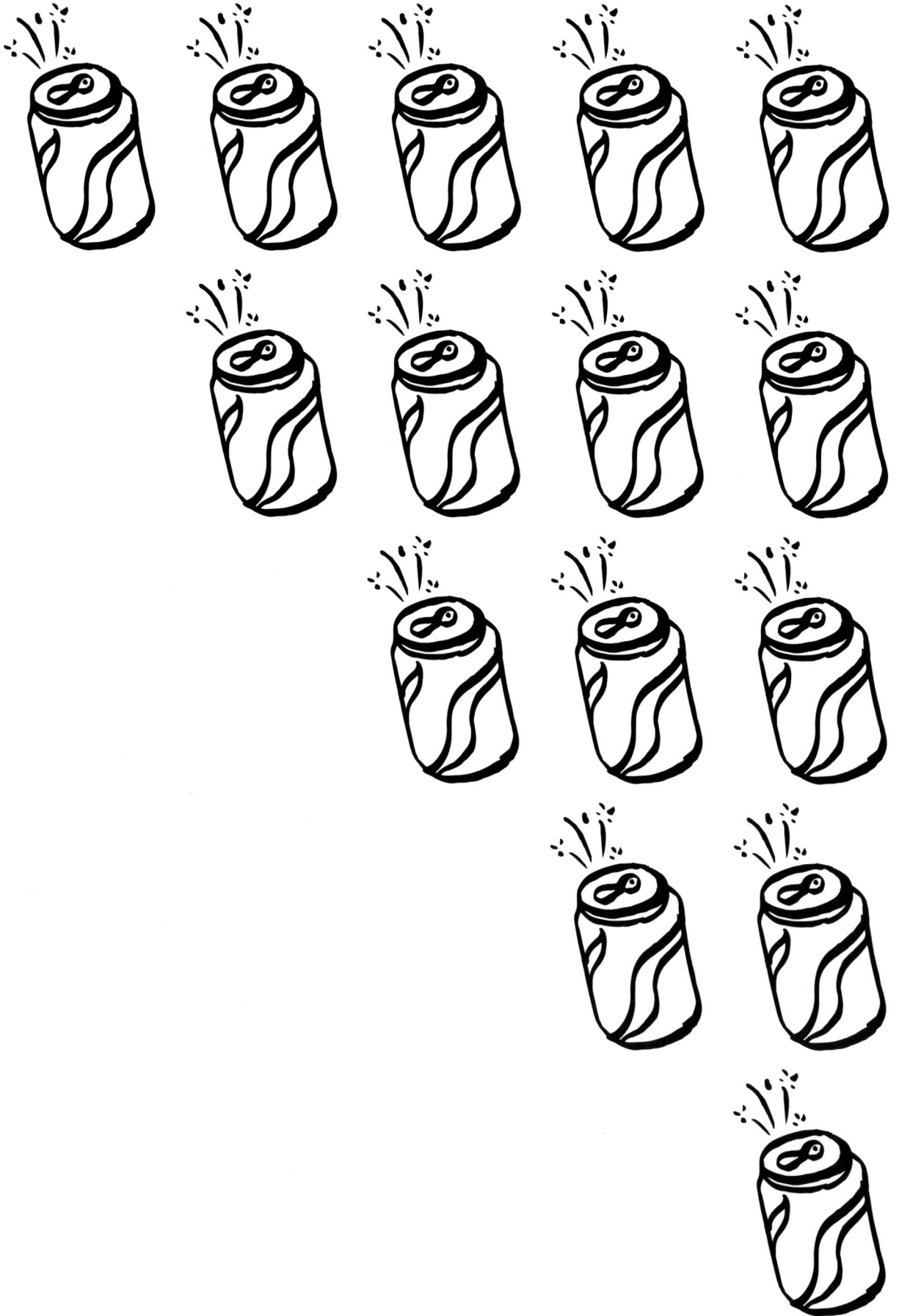

YEAR 6
Numbers and the number system

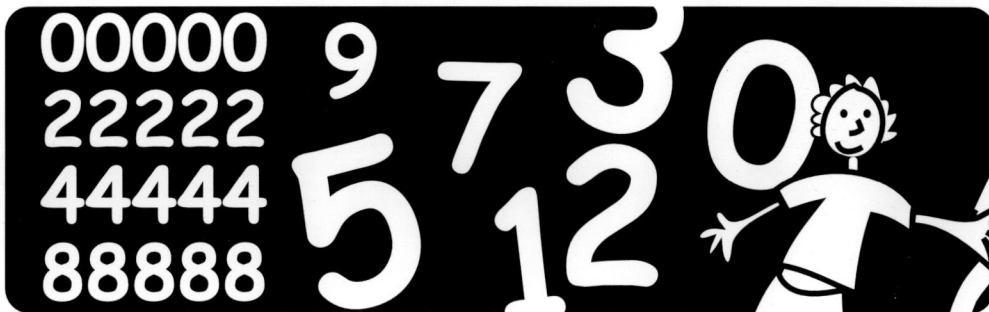

00000
22222
44444
88888
9 7 5 3 0
5 12

Objective
Numbers and the number system
Multiply and divide decimals mentally by 10 or 100 and explain the effect.

Instruction
Count the amount of money you have in your money-box or ask someone at home if you can count the amount of money they have in their purse. Write that down e.g. £6.34. Then write down what there would be if there was 10 times as much, then 100 times as much.

Then go back to the original amount. Write down what there would be if there was a tenth of that, then a hundredth of that.

Back in school
The children must think what they could buy with the different amounts to help develop their sense of the value of money.

. . . .

Objective
Number and the number system
Use the vocabulary of estimation and approximation. Consolidate rounding an integer to the nearest 10, 100 or 1000.

Instruction
Round your telephone number or a friend's telephone number to the nearest 1000. Write down the number and what it rounds to.

Back in school
Work in pairs to round each other's numbers to the nearest 100 and to the nearest 10.

. . . .

Numbers and the number system
Find the difference between a positive and a negative integer or two negative integers, in a context such as temperature, and order a set of positive and negative integers.

Instruction
Look in a daily paper and find the section which tells you the temperatures from different towns around the world. Write them out in order from the hottest to the coldest.

Then work out the difference between the hottest and coldest town in the world.

Back in school
Compare the temperatures in different places. Which is the hottest place the children found? Which is the coldest?

. . . .

Objective
Numbers and the number system
Recognise and extend number sequences.

Instruction
Make up a rule for a sequence of numbers, e.g. double it and add one. How far can you get with extending your sequence in 15 minutes? Bring the sequence back to school.

Back in school
Children work in fours. Can they guess the rule for the other children's sequences?

. . . .

Objective
Number and the number system
Make general statements about odd or even numbers, including the outcome of products.

Instruction
Remind the children that:
E + E = E
O + O = E
O + E = O
when O = an odd number and E = an even number.
Ask them to make up a rule for multiplication of odd and even numbers and think of examples to prove it.

Teacher's note: you could tell some of the more able children that they must use two-digit numbers for their proof and the less able that they can use single digit numbers.

Back in school
What about division? Or subtraction? Discuss these in school.

. . . .

Objective
Numbers and the number system
Know and apply simple tests of divisibility. Find simple common multiples.

Instruction
Write down your telephone number (or the school's). Use your knowledge of tests of divisibility to work out whether it is a multiple of 2, 3, 4, 5, 6, 8, 9, 10, 25 and 100.

Back in school
Compare numbers. Whose number is a prime number? Is anyone's number divisible by several numbers?

. . . .

Objective
Numbers and the number system
Reduce a fraction to its simplest form by cancelling common factors in the numerator and the denominator.
Change a fraction to the equivalent mixed number and vice versa.

Instruction
Write down your age in years and completed months, e.g. 10 years 4 months. Then write this as a fraction:

$$10 \, ^4/_{12}$$

Now, if possible, reduce this to its simplest form:

$$10^1/_3$$

Now write it as an improper fraction:

$$^{31}/_3$$

Do this for some other people in your family.

Back in school
Compare fractions. Which fractions couldn't be reduced to a simple form? Make an 'age ladder' for the class, putting the children's names on it in order.

....

Objective
Number and the number system
Use a fraction as an 'operator' to find fractions, including tenths and hundredths, of numbers or quantities.

Instruction
Find a recipe where the quantities given are for four people. Work out how much of each ingredient you would need if you made it for three people instead. How about for five people?

Back in school
Plan for and then make some of the recipes!

....

Objective
Numbers and the number system
Order fractions and position them on a number line.

Instruction
Take the last three or four digits of your phone number (or the school's phone number). Use the digits to make fractions less than one, e.g. digits 2, 5, 7 make $^2/_5$, $^2/_7$, $^5/_7$.
Draw a number line and position these fractions on it.

Teacher's note: there will be three possible fractions if there are three different digits and six possible combinations if there are four different digits.

You can ask children to make all possible fractions and draw an appropriate number line to position them on.

Back in school
Discuss who made the largest fraction? The smallest fraction? The fraction closest to $^1/_2$? To $^1/_4$?, etc.

....

Objective
Number and the number system
Use a fraction as an 'operator' to find fractions, including tenths and hundredths, of numbers or quantities.

Instruction
Make up some puzzles for the class to solve where the answer is a number and the clues you give involve fractions, e.g. Two-thirds of the number I am thinking of is 50. What is the number? (75).
Three-tenths of the money in my money-box is 21p. How much money have I got in it? (70p)
I'm thinking of a number; it is $^7/_8$ of 40. What is the number? (35)
Write your best one down and bring it into school.

Back in school
The children can work in fours and help each other work out each others' puzzles.

YEAR 6 Y6

Objective
Number and the number system
Solve simple problems involving ratio and proportion.

Instruction
Look in your local paper. Work out what proportion of the paper is concerned with sport or house sales or motoring? Write that as a proportion. Then write it as a ratio.

Back in school
Compare answers. Did several children use the same paper? Did they get several different answers? Discuss how we can get to an accurate ratio?

. . . .

Objective
Numbers and the number system
Solve simple problems involving ratio and proportion.

Instruction
Find something in your house that you can express as a ratio. Here are some examples:
In the fruit bowl there are 3 apples for every 2 oranges.
In my money-box/someone's purse there are 3 copper coins for every 8 silver coins.
In the cupboard there are 2 packets of plain crisps for every 5 flavoured crisps.

Back in school
Use this as the start of the maths lesson to make up statements based on what you have found.

Teacher's note: see National Numeracy Strategy Framework page 27, Section 6 for examples of statements.

. . . .

Objective
Number and the number system,
and
Measures, shape and space
Use decimal notation for tenths, hundredths and thousandths when recording measurements.
Know what each digit represents in a number with up to three decimal places.
Order a mixed set of numbers or measurements with up to three decimal places.

Instruction
Look for three things in your house which have got their weight written on them. Write down the weight as expressed on the label then write it in another form using decimals, e.g. 454g, 0.454kg. Then put the decimal fractions you have made in order of size.

Teacher's note: you could do the same activity, but using capacity (litres) or length (e.g. metres).

Back in school
Compare weights. The children work in groups of four to order their weights.

. . . .

Objective
Numbers and the number system
Find simple percentages of whole numbers.

Instruction
Find an advert for a house in the local free paper. Pretend you own it and want to sell it. Estate agents usually charge 2% to sell it for you. Work out how much they will charge you to sell your dream house!

Teacher's note: if this is too difficult for some of the children you could tell them that some of them got a bargain and the estate agent is only charging them 1%!

Back in school
Compare the house prices. Which houses seem to be very good value? Discuss what factors you will take into account in making your judgement e.g. area, number of rooms, state of house, etc.

Y6
YEAR 6

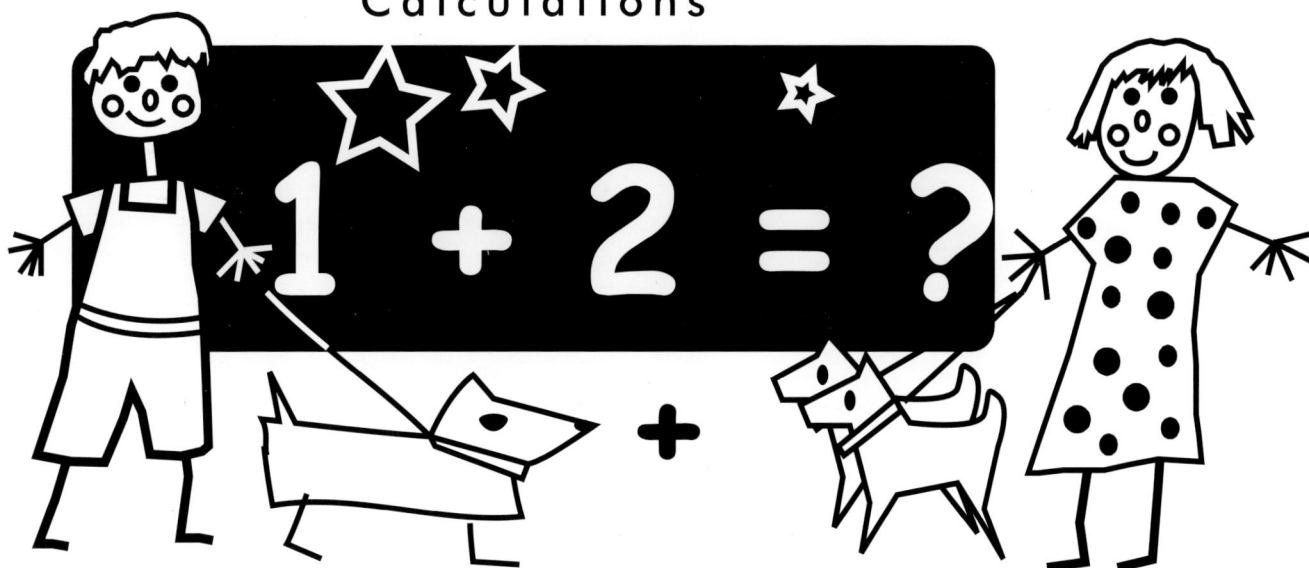

From Barbara Teffer, Highfield JI School

Objective
Calculations
Use known number facts and place value to consolidate mental addition.

Instruction
Build your own number wall.

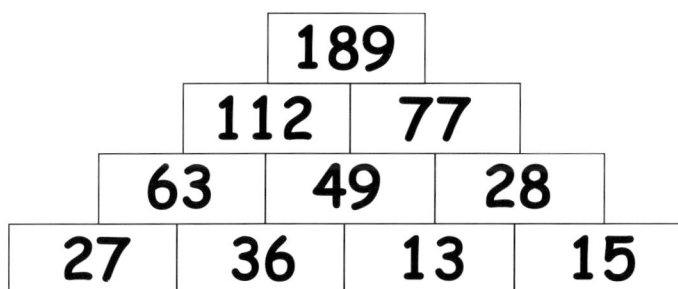

Teacher's note: you can specify the number of digits that you want the children to put in the bottom layer and also the height of the wall. This can also be done using decimal numbers.

Back in school
Specify the number of bricks and write a top number. The children work in pairs to construct a wall that works!

Objective
Calculations
Understand and use the relationships between the four operations and use brackets.

Instruction
Using the last five digits of your telephone number (or the school's telephone number) and any of the four operations can you make all the numbers from 1-25?

Back in school
Write each number from 1-25 on the board and ask the children to suggest different ways of making each one.

. . . .

YEAR 6 **Y6**

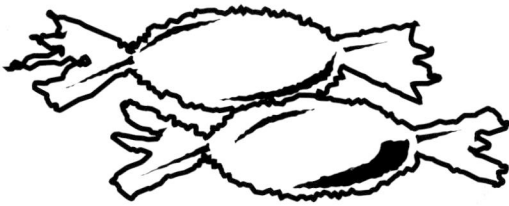

Objective
Calculations

Divide £.p. by a two-digit number then round up or down as appropriate.

Instruction

Find out the price of your favourite sweet. See how much money you have in your money-box. Work out how many of that sweet you could buy?

Back in school

Write an amount on the board, e.g. £5. How many sweets could you buy for this amount?

. . . .

Objective
Calculations

Consolidate knowing by heart multiplication facts up to 10 x 10.

Instruction

Decide which is the multiplication table that you are least sure of. Choose up to three facts within that table, e.g. 7 x 7, 5 x 7, 9 x 7. Make up a rhyme to help you learn each of those facts.

Teacher's note: you may need to help the children choose which facts to learn. Point out to them that if they learn, for example, 7 x 7 then they should be able to work out 8 x 7 quickly.

Back in school

Share each other's rhymes. Perhaps three or four children can put theirs together to make a song?

. . . .

Objective
Calculations

Derive quickly doubles of two-digit numbers.

Instruction

Tear a piece of paper into ten pieces and write the numbers 0-9 on them. Turn them over. Ask an adult or an older brother or sister to play against you. Turn over two of the numbers to make a two-digit number. Can you beat the adult at doubling the number? Sometimes make the number a decimal number instead of a whole number e.g. 4.8 instead of 48.

Back in school

Put the children in pairs to play. They try to beat each other by being the fastest!

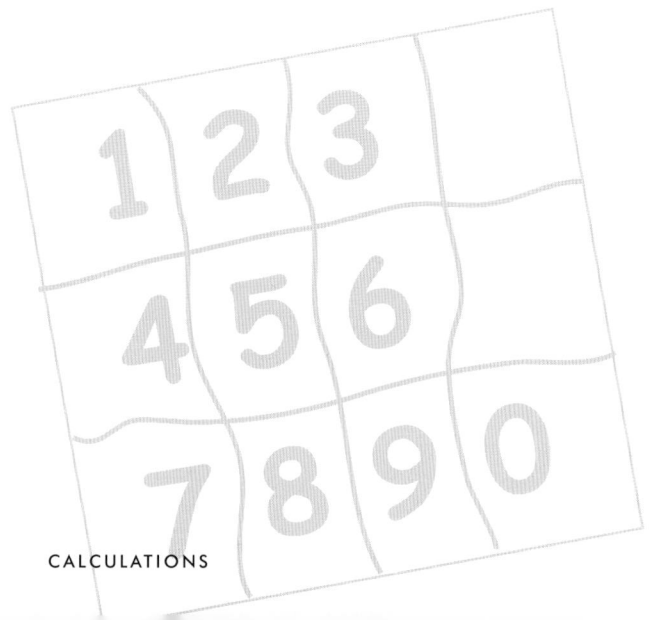

. . . .

Objective
Calculations

Derive quickly halves of multiples of 10 to 1000, e.g. 670 ÷ 2.

Instruction

Tear a piece of paper into ten pieces and write the numbers 0-9 on them. Turn them over. Ask an adult or an older brother or sister to play against you. Turn over two of the numbers to make a two-digit number but make it ten times bigger, i.e. 67 becomes 670. Then can you beat the adult at halving the number?

Back in school

Put the children in pairs to play. They try to beat each other by being the fastest!

Y6

Objective
Calculations
Derive quickly doubles of multiples of 100 to 10,000, e.g. 6500 x 2.

Instruction
Tear a piece of paper into ten pieces and write the numbers 0-9 on them. Turn them over. Ask an adult or an older brother or sister to play against you. Turn over two of the numbers to make a two-digit number but make it a hundred times bigger i.e. 65 becomes 6500. Then can you beat the adult at doubling the number?

Back in school
Put the children in pairs to play. They try to beat each other by being the fastest!

· · · · · · · ·

Objective
Calculations
Use related facts and doubling (or halving). For example, find the 24 times table by doubling the 6 times table twice.

Instruction
Show an adult how you can work out, for example, the 24 times table by doubling the six times table twice. Then choose a table for the adult to work out in the same way. Who is better at it you or the adult?

Teacher's note: you might want to discuss with the children which tables are appropriate to ask an adult to work out, i.e. using the double rule with a number that is a multiple of 4.

Back in school
Compare tables. The children work in fours to ask each other really hard questions from their table, e.g. 6 x 24!

· · · · · · · ·

Objective
Calculations
Use closely related facts e.g. multiply by 29 or 31 by multiplying by 30 and adjusting. Use the relationship between multiplication and addition or multiplication and division.

Instruction
Give the children a number fact, e.g. 30 x 16 = 480. Ask them to work out what else they can work out through knowing that fact.
Obviously this is not confined to just knowing 29 and 31 x 16, but also 60, 15, 300, 0.3 x 16 etc, and also related division facts.

Back in school
Compare your facts. Make a comprehensive list on the board.

· · · · · · · ·

Objective
Calculations
Paper and pencil procedures. Develop and refine written methods for multiplication. Use the relationship between multiplication and division.

Instruction
Work out approximately how much you spent on sweets last week. Using that information work out how much you probably spend on sweets in a year. When you have done that, use that information to make up a division problem for your friend to solve in the lesson, e.g. I will probably spend £70.20 on sweets this year. How much will I spend each week? (£1.35)

Back in school
The children work in pairs to solve each other's division problem.

Teacher's note: this can lead on to a decision about whether to use a calculator to solve a problem.

· · · · · · · ·

YEAR 6 **Y6**

From Geoff Griffiths

Calculations

Approximate first. Use informal pencil and paper methods to support and record multiplication calculations.

Instruction

What would happen if you multiplied each digit of a phone number in turn? What do you think the final answer would be? For example, my phone number is 2465152 so that's 2 x 4 = 8, 8 x 6 = 48, 48 x 5 = 240 and so on.
Estimate what your answer will be then find out how close you were.

Back in school

Compare answers. What is the range? What is the largest possible answer with a six- or seven-digit phone number? What is the smallest possible answer?

. . . .

2465152

2 x 4 = 8

8 x 6 = 48

48 x 5 = 240

240 x 1 = 240

240 x 5 = 1200

1200 x 2 = 2400

Y6

Solving problems

how do I...

Objective
Solving problems
Choose and use appropriate number operations to solve problems and appropriate ways of calculating.

Instruction
Make up some sums, and find the answers, using all four operations. You can use brackets too if you want. Then write them out without putting in the operation used. Bring them to school for the class to solve at the beginning of the maths lesson, e.g.

453 * 4 = 1812	453 * 259 = 712
453 * 5 = 90.6	453 * 259 = 194

Back in school
Use the children's work to generate the mental/oral starter to your lesson.

. . . .

From Barbara Teffer, Highfield JI School

Objective
Solving problems
Investigate a general statement by finding examples that satisfy it.
Recognise prime numbers (to at least 20).

Instruction
It is said that you can make every even number (except 2) up to 100 by adding two prime numbers. Is it true?

Teacher's note: *you could split this up between different ability groups in the class e.g. lower ability number 4-30, middle ability 31-55 and 56-79, higher ability 80-100.*

Back in school
Compare your findings. Is the conjecture true?

. . . .

YEAR 6 **Y6**

From Barbara Teffer, Highfield JI School

Objective
Solving problems
Investigate a general statement by finding examples that satisfy it.
Recognise prime numbers (to at least 20).

Instruction
It is said that all odd numbers are the sum of three prime numbers. Is it true?

Teacher's note: you could split this up between different ability groups in the class, e.g. lower ability number 4-30, middle ability 31-55 and 56-79, higher ability 80-100.)

Back in school
Compare your findings. Is the conjecture true?

. . . .

Objective
Solving problems
Identify and use appropriate operations to solve word problems involving numbers and quantities.

Instruction
Ask your mum, dad or carer roughly how much they spend on food (or in the supermarket) in a week. Using that information work out how much they spend in a year.

Back in school
Discuss the twenty most crucial items of food a family needs each week. Write the approximate price of each one and work out the total cost.

. . . .

Objective
Solving problems
Identify and use appropriate operations to solve word problems involving numbers and quantities.

Instruction
Find out the usual size of your favourite packet of cereal, e.g. 250g, 500g, etc. Ask roughly how long a box lasts your family. Work out the total weight of that cereal your family eats in a year. Then work out if that is more or less than you weigh!

Back in school
Compare weights then write all the weights in order.

. . . .

Objective
Solving problems
Identify and use appropriate operations to solve word problems involving numbers and quantities.

Instruction
Find out the capacity of the containers of soft drink that you usually have in your house. Ask your mum or carer how many of those your family usually get through in a week. Then work out approximately what capacity of that drink your family gets through in a month. How do you think that compares with the capacity of your bath?

Back in school
Compare capacities. Write all the quantities in order.

. . . .

Y6

Objective
Solving problems
Use all four operations to solve word problems involving time.

Instruction
Find out what times the sun rises and sets this week. Work out how many hours and minutes of daylight there are each day.

Back in school
Discuss how the hours of daylight change. What factors affect them: where you are, time of year, etc.

. . . .

Objective
Solving problems
Use all four operations to solve word problems involving time.

Instruction
Keep a time diary of about a six-hour period in any day you choose between now and when the homework has to be returned. Try to make it as precise as you can, e.g.
4.27 p.m. began to play a game
5.14 p.m. finished game and began tea
5.35 p.m. began to watch Neighbours
6.08 p.m. began homework

Back in school
Make up some time problems for others in the class to solve.
Think about asking some two-step problems too, e.g. How much longer do I spend playing a game than watching Neighbours?

. . . .

From J. Brown and J. Evans, Kings Norton Primary School

Objective
Solving problems
Identify and use appropriate operations (including combinations of operations) to solve word problems involving numbers and quantities.
Find simple percentages of small whole number quantities (by halving).

Instruction
Look through a local paper or magazine. Find something you would like to buy. Estimate its price without VAT. Justify your estimate at 17.5%.

Back in school
The children work in fours to check each others' estimates.

. . . .

Handling data

Objective

Handling data

Solve a problem by extracting and interpreting data in tables, graphs, and charts.

Instruction

Find examples of data being represented in a table, graph or chart. Look in the newspapers, brochures, leaflets, reference books, atlases, or on computers.

Decide what the table, graph or chart is showing, copy or cut it out to bring in, and then prepare a question to ask the class about it.

Back in school

The children work in pairs to study each other's charts and answer the questions.

· · · · · · · ·

Objective

Handling data

Find the mode and range of a set of data. Begin to find the median and the mean.

Instruction

Look in a daily paper and find the section which tells you the temperatures from different towns in Britain. Find the range and the mode. Then work out the median.

Back in school

Compare the different modes, and also the medians. How close is the mode to each median? How do the different medians compare? Why are some higher than others?

7°C

17°C

19°C

11°C

12°C

9°C

10°C

16°C

Measures, shape and space

Measures, shape and space
Estimate using metric units (length).

Instruction
Think of something that is about 1 metre long and write it down. Then something that is about 10 metres long.
Then 100 metres long.
Then 1000 metres long (a kilometre).
Then 10,000 metres long.
Then 100,000 metres long.
Then 1,000,000 metres long.

Instruction 2
(This could be used for the next homework.)
Think of something 1 metre long.
Then one tenth of a metre long.
Then one hundredth of a metre long (one centimetre).
Then one thousandth of a metre long (one millimetre).
Then one thousandth of a centimetre long!

Back in school
Each child chooses an example to draw. Make a display of their drawings in different length categories.

....

Objective
Measures, shape and space
Estimate using metric units (weight).

Instruction
As with estimation of length. You may want to use the idea of increasing and decreasing by the power of 10 as one homework, but perhaps not go so far in each direction.

Back in school
Each child chooses an example to draw. Make a display of their drawings in different weight categories.

....

YEAR 6 Y6

Objective
Measures, shape and space
Estimate using metric units (capacity).

Instruction
As for weight and length. You might want to limit how far they go in either direction. On the other hand it would be a challenge!

Back in school
Each child chooses an example to draw. Make a display of their drawings in different capacity categories.

. . . .

From St. Peter's CE School, Harborne

Objective
Measures, shape and space
Measure and calculate the perimeter and area of simple shapes.

Instruction
Measure the perimeter and work out the floor area of one of the rooms in your house.

Back in school
Work out what shape the room could be to give a larger or smaller area with the same perimeter, or the same area with a larger or smaller perimeter.

. . . .

Objective
Measures, shape and space
Describe and visualise 2D and 3D shapes.

Instruction
Fold a piece of A4 paper in half. On the inside draw a simple 'picture' using three or four tangram pieces. Then, on the outside of the paper give instructions for making the picture

Back in school
Work in pairs to solve each other's problems.

From Barbara Teffer, Highfield JI School

Objective
Measures, shape and space
Recognise reflective symmetry in 2D shapes, reflections and translations.

Instruction
Make your own pattern showing reflection in two mirror lines at right angles (see National Numeracy Strategy Framework, section 6 page 107) or using translation.

Back in school
Display the best examples of patterns.

. . . .

Objective
Measures, Shape and Space
Recognise and estimate angles.

Instruction
Make a list of or draw items in, say, the kitchen or garage with turning parts, e.g. garden shears, tin opener, door hinge, scissors, windows. Then decide, when they are fully open, if the angle that it turned is acute, obtuse or reflex. Estimate the size of the angle.

Back in school
Categorise the angles under headings: right angles, acute, obtuse, or reflex.

. . . .

Y6